MIDDLESBROUGH

Albert Park

HISTORY, HERITAGE & RESTORATION

COMPILED BY

NORMAN MOORSOM
MA, ACP, DIP ED

Wharncliffe Books

Dedicated to Ray Cleeton of Ripon
and to the memory of his great-grandfather,
Edward Cleaton,
the first Curator of Albert Park

**First Published in 2002 by arrangement with
Wharncliffe Books**
an imprint of
**Pen and Sword Books Limited,
47 Church Street, Barnsley,
South Yorkshire. S70 2AS**

Copyright © Norman Moorsom 2002

For up-to-date information on other titles produced under the
Wharncliffe imprint, please telephone or write to:

> **Wharncliffe Books
> FREEPOST
> 47 Church Street
> Barnsley
> South Yorkshire S70 2BR
> Telephone (24 hours): 01226 - 734555**

ISBN: 1-903425-22-0

A CIP catalogue record of this book is available from the
British Library

Cover illustration: Italian Walk, c1871. Teesside Archives Department

Printed in the United Kingdom by
CPI UK

Contents

You are invited to visit Albert Park, to enjoy its sights and sounds, its airy acres and its recreational facilities. Take this volume with you as a guide to its history and its restoration. Photo George Ward

Foreword

by Ken Sherwood

One significant fact which stands out in the following text is that Middlesbrough's Albert Park has played a very important part in the life of the town for more than 130 years. I am proud to say that the Park was also a significant feature of my own life for over forty years, during which time I was able to make a personal contribution towards its upkeep and development.

I was born in Middlesbrough in 1929 and joined the Albert Park workforce as an apprentice gardener in 1943, at the age of fourteen. I was called up into the Army to do my National Service from 1947 to 1949 and when I came back, I worked in Albert Park again for a few months, before becoming a chargehand with a gang of four men at Nunthorpe Hall. At that time, it was being altered from the Ardencaple Maternity Home to an Old People's Home, the first in Middlesbrough. From there, I moved to Stewart Park as a foreman gardener and then I was made Head Gardener for Stewart Park and outside areas, which involved laying out new housing estates.

After that, I was made Area Supervisor, which included responsibility for the grassed areas at Teesside Airport, also maintaining other grassed areas, farmland and farm crops. In Teesside County Borough from 1968 to 1974, I was Area Superintendent for the whole of Middlesbrough and for Thornaby. In 1974, the year in which Cleveland County was established, I was appointed Parks Manager for Middlesbrough, by which time the level of staffing had increased greatly. In 1989, I was appointed as Horticultural Adviser to the Parks Department for a year, helping with the re-structuring of the Department. I retired in August 1990, after forty-six-and-a half years' service with the Council. Soon after my retirement, I was honoured to receive my British Empire Medal.

Just before I retired, Norman Moorsom and his colleague from the Archives Department interviewed me several times in order to record memories of my working life and it is very satisfying to be able to read some of my own stories in his book. I am particularly pleased to have the opportunity of writing the Foreword for this book, which I feel is a valuable record of the history and heritage of Albert Park. I am also very pleased to see that readers are actively encouraged to go into the Park in order to see it all for themselves.

With my own intimate knowledge of the Park, I am delighted to see that it is being restored to its former splendour and I sincerely hope that visitors will treat it with respect.

Middlesbrough
March 2002

Preface

During the course of a holiday on the lovely Greek island of Rhodes in the Autumn of 2001, my wife, Sylvia, and I decided to visit the highly-acclaimed Rodini Park, in Rhodes Town. In view of the great expectations which had been raised by the tourist literature, we were both distinctly underwhelmed by what we actually discovered on our tour of inspection. The main impression which we took away with us was one of gratitude for Albert Park and Stewart Park, back home in Middlesbrough. It is often the case that you do not fully appreciate what is right on your own doorstep until you have compared it with similar features elsewhere.

There can be very few Middlesbrough residents, whether home-grown or imported, who do not have a tale or two to tell about memories of, or associations with, Albert Park.

My older sister, Rita, and I were often taken to the Park in the 1940s and 1950s, then Sylvia and I took along our own two children, Richard and Hilary in the 1960s and 1970s. We are now enjoying the same routine with our two grandchildren, Laura and Andrew, albeit less frequently and at a much more sedate pace. For me, there is no escaping the sheer pleasure, both physical and nostalgic, of being in the Park and for that reason alone I was particularly pleased to become personally involved in a very significant project associated with it.

In 1997, Middlesbrough Borough Council made a bid for Heritage Lottery funding as a means of restoring the Park to its Victorian glory. As the basis of this bid, it was necessary to provide a document which detailed the history and heritage of the Park itself, in order to demonstrate its long-standing and on-going significance to the townsfolk for whose benefit it had been created 130 years earlier. I was commissioned to compile this document and found it to be a most interesting undertaking in itself.

Having grown up in Middlesbrough and always accepted the fact that Albert Park was there for the enjoyment of residents and visitors of all ages, the research project proved to be most enlightening. For me, it had never been a matter of familiarity breeding contempt, but it did become clear that it had been very easy to take the Park for granted as a feature of local life which must always have been there.

Since I became much more aware of the background to the design and creation of the Park, and its subsequent evolution and maintenance, I find that family visits are even more enjoyable. It is a simple matter of appreciating the continuity of shared experiences and the feeling of, quite literally, being able to follow in the footsteps of my local forebears. Although much has changed in the Park over the years, it still acts as a magnet for all generations of families who wish to relax on a bench, to let off steam in the open spaces and the playground area, to have a row around the boating lake, or to add to the waistline problems of the ever-popular ducks and other resident waterfowl.

Based on my original researches, the aim of this volume is threefold: to provide sufficient material to satisfy the curiosity of those with a real interest in local history, whether as students or as leisure-time readers, to act as a stimulus for pure nostalgia in re-visiting the park itself, and to encourage those who have never set foot within its boundaries to do just that.

My historical material has been gleaned from a number of contemporary sources, and wherever possible I have allowed them to speak for themselves in my text. These include newspaper articles and reports and the minutes of the Park Committee, the latter having been analysed from their beginnings in 1868. I have also considered legal documents associated with the gift of land for the actual creation of the Park.

I believe that there is nothing more fascinating than being able to listen to the voice of the past and for those readers who would like to experience the full flavour of Victorian journalistic descriptions of the Park, I have included in my Appendices a number of lengthy newspaper articles from the period 1868 to 1883. By the same token, if you do not wish to become immersed in such detail, simply ignore them.

I hope that you will enjoy browsing through the following pages and that you will feel inspired, if you are able, to link it with a walk round the Park itself. If it is your first visit, you are in for a real treat, and if it is the latest of many visits you will be able to compare your earliest memories with your impressions of new and improved features.

As is often the case, the completion of one writing project leads to plans for the next, and here you may be able to help me. I intend to compile an account of the on-going work of restoration in the Park, to be published at the time of the completion of Phase Two, and I would very much like to link this text with a body of material based on the memories and anecdotes of both residents and visitors. You may be in a position to pass on to me a whole series of anecdotes from your own memory-bank, or to lend me post cards or family snaps, which could be copied and returned. If this is the case I will be delighted to hear from you at the address below.

Norman Moorsom
5, Levisham Close,
Acklam,
Middlesbrough
TS5 7LT

April 2002

Acknowledgements

I am very grateful to my wife Sylvia and my son Richard for their help in preparing and proof-reading my text, which I always find to be a difficult task.

My thanks are also due to the individuals and bodies listed below for their assistance with information and copyright illustrations. The source of each illustration is noted with it. Every effort has been made to trace other copyright-holders, but with no success.

Jeremy Alder, Middlesbrough Libraries & Information; Ken Barlow, Acklam, Middlesbrough; Birkenhead Reference Library; Tansee Cartwright, Albert Park Development Officer; Ray Cleeton, Ripon; Marion Coles, Linthorpe, Middlesbrough: Dorman Museum, Middlesbrough; Derek Enderby, Marton, Middlesbrough; The Friends of Albert Park; John Goodchild, Wakefield; Halifax Reference Library; Barbara Harrison, Acklam, Middlesbrough; Jack Hatfield, Great Ayton; Hirst Conservation, Sleaford; The Illustrated London News Picture Library; David Kelsey, Linthorpe, Middlesbrough; Landscape Design Associates, Peterborough; Leeds Reference Library; Sheila Metcalf, Bath; Middlesbrough Council Transport & Design Services; Middlesbrough Reference Library; Newcastle Reference Library; Gordon Newton, Marton, Middlesbrough; Ken Sherwood, Brookfield, Middlesbrough; Mr A Stephenson, South Bank, Middlesbrough; Paul Stephenson, Linthorpe, Middlesbrough; Sunderland Reference Library; Teesside Archives Department, Middlesbrough; Wakefield Reference Library; George Ward, Ormesby, Middlesbrough.

Suggested Reading

1. Chadwick, George F, The Park and the Town - Public Landscape in the 19th and 20th Centuries (1966).
2. Green, Fiona, A Guide to the Historic Parks and Gardens of Tyne and Wear (1995).
3. Lillie, William, History of Middlesbrough (1968).
4. Metcalf, Sheila, Albert Park - A Place for the Recreation of the People (In Bulletin 38 of the Cleveland and Teesside Local History Society, 1980).
5. Moorsom, Norman, A Journey Through the History of Middlesbrough (1993).
6. Pattenden, David W, Horticulture in Mid-19th Century Middlesbrough (In Bulletin 40 of the Cleveland and Teesside Local History Society, 1981).
7. Polley, Linda, The Other Middlesbrough: A Study of Three 19th Century Suburbs (1993): Albert Park Supplementary Research Report (2000).
8. Reid, H G, Middlesbrough and its Institutions: With a Record of the Opening of the Albert Park by HRH Prince Arthur (1868).
9. Various: Middlesbrough, Its History, Environs and Trade, (1898).

Chapter One

Historical Background and Origins

Historical Significance

The full significance of the life of any individual, of any event or of any subject may be appreciated more fully when it is considered within its wider historical context. This is true of Middlesbrough's Albert Park, the background to the establishing of which highlights its importance in the life of the citizens of the expanding industrial urban community. A simple fact which may be stated at the outset is that it proved to be a unique boon to the town-dwellers in the northern area of original settlement and that it led to the expansion of the suburb of New Linthorpe to the south.

Middlesbrough's Industrial Background

The town of Middlesbrough was established in 1830, thirty-eight years before the official opening of Albert Park. It owed its existence directly to the activities of the proprietors of the Stockton & Darlington Railway, a business concern which had become operational in 1825. Their principal aim was to transport coal from pits in the Auckland area of County Durham to centres of population like Stockton and Darlington in the south of the County. In the following year they inaugurated the second phase of their business plan, which was to export trade from specially-constructed staiths at the port of Stockton.

Problems associated with the nature of the river Tees in terms of difficult navigation from the estuary to Stockton and its shallowness at the staiths led the promoters to look further east for an export outlet. They decided to establish a new shipping-place closer to the estuary on the south bank of the River Tees, where it was naturally deeper. This was close to the tiny agricultural community of Middlesbrough and the facility was known as *Port Darlington*, from where the first cargo of coal was shipped on 27 December 1830.

During the following decade, other industries were established in the specially-created town of Middlesbrough, which was in itself the first urban offspring of the railway system. These included a shipyard in 1833 and a pottery in the following year, but it was not until 1841 that the major breakthrough occurred, with the opening of the Middlesbrough Ironworks,

Henry William Ferdinand Bolckow and John Vaughan, co-founders of Middlesbrough's first Iron Works in 1841. Author's Collection

enry William Ferdinand Bolckow

John Vaughan

Bolckow and Vaughan's Middlesbrough Iron Works, situated east of the town and producing considerable atmospheric pollution for its residents. Author's Collection

established by Henry William Ferdinand Bolckow and John Vaughan.

The discovery in 1850 of a deposit of ironstone at Eston proved to be crucial, in that it did away with the inconvenient necessity of transporting ore from the Whitby area by sea, then the construction of furnaces at Middlesbrough in 1852 solved another problem. From that time, it was no longer necessary to take the local ore for initial processing at the firm's furnaces at Witton Park in County Durham. It was the iron, and later steel, trade which really established Middlesbrough as an important centre of heavy industry, with both a national and an international reputation.

Middlesbrough's Social Background

The dormitory town of Middlesbrough had been created on the green-field site of the Middlesbrough Farm by an independent consortium of six Quaker partners, under the direction of Joseph Pease of Darlington, who were known as the Owners of the Middlesbrough Estate. The first house in the town was actually erected in West Street in April 1830. The original area set aside as the site for the town consisted of thirty acres of farmland and it is a surprising fact that this was less than half the area of Albert Park itself.

Even when it was well established in the 1850s, the town itself was still confined to the area between the river and the railway line to Redcar, which had been opened in 1846. The rapid industrial explosion and southern urban expansion of the following decade had a dramatic effect upon population and housing density in the town, with living conditions leaving a great deal to be desired due to the practice of running in mile after mile of terraced dwellings as close as possible to the growing number of works.

Joseph Pease of Darlington, the Founder of modern Middlesbrough, who encouraged the establishing of the town's early industries. Author's Collection

In the early days, Middlesbrough's population was predominantly male in gender and the basic social problem facing the community was that of an over-indulgence in the consumption of alcohol. A Temperance Society was established in 1834 and beyond that there was a more widely-based bid to encourage involvement in activities of a more wholesome and cultural nature than that of spending time, and hard-earned

Densely-packed terraced housing from the mid-Victorian period of Middlesbrough's rapid development. Middlesbrough Reference Library

wages, in a public house or a beerhouse. For those who cared to take advantage of them, there existed a variety of group and society activities, with or without religious associations. However, one crucial factor could not be evaded – that of the environment, which was pervaded by the fall-out of heavy industry.

A Private Park and Public Opinion

In spite of the adverse environmental conditions which existed in the riverside area of the town at the time of its major industrial revolution, an early attempt had been made by Richard Jowsey, a local businessman, to brighten the lives of Middlesbrough folk through the establishing of pleasure grounds. These were situated between two of the railway tracks leading to the coal staiths at the Middlesbrough Dock. What was, in effect, Middlesbrough's first park was described in the following glowing terms in the *Darlington and Stockton Times* of 12 July 1856:

> ....*Mr Richard Jowsey, who during the leisure hours of the day, with the assistance of his men, has laid out, cultivated, beautified and changed this once barren spot to as delightful a retreat and pleasure ground as any in this part of the country. The place is planted with rows of poplars, larch, etc. which have grown to large and stately trees: a beautiful grotto adorned with shells, and the figureheads of warriors and naval heroes, stands prominent amidst the serpentine gravel walks: a magnificent eagle within its own spacious boundary is elevated on a lofty perch ready to devour any of the feathered tribe; goats, peacocks, etc. perambulate grassy plains, and at the entrance is erected for the musicians of Middlesbrough a lofty stand or platform where the band plays in the evenings, and at the farthest end of the walks is a sheet of water enclosed, which is ultimately to be the abode of choice and rare fish.*

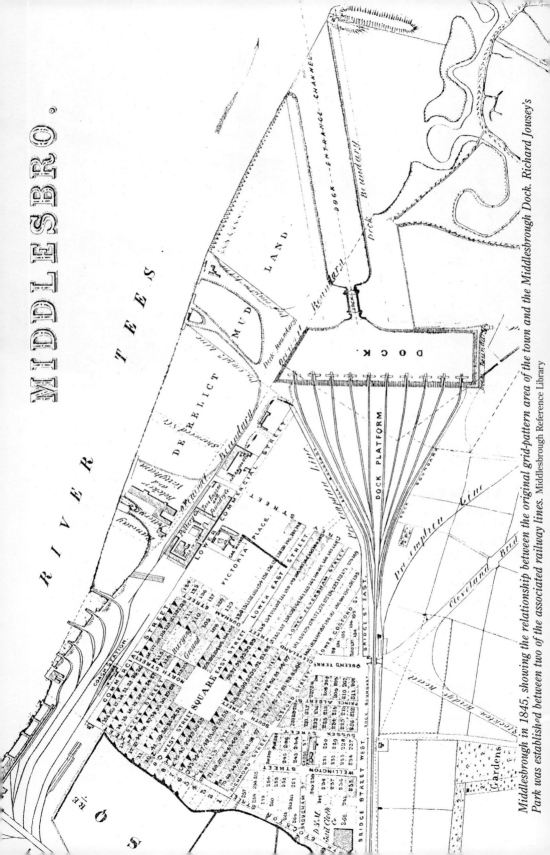

MIDDLESBRO'.

RIVER TEES

MUD LAND

DOCK

DOCK ENTRANCE CHANNEL

DOCK PLATFORM

Middlesbrough in 1845, showing the relationship between the original grid-pattern area of the town and the Middlesbrough Dock. Richard Jowsey's Park was established between two of the associated railway lines. Middlesbrough Reference Library

There is no indication as to the date of the actual creation of the privately-promoted Jowsey Park, but it can be deduced from the reference to well-established trees that it must have been several years prior to 1856, unless, of course, the trees were mature at the time of planting.

In 1859, possibly inspired by Richard Jowsey's example, the desirability of a *People's Park* was being considered by Middlesbrough Town Council and the following interesting account appeared in the columns of the *Middlesbrough Weekly News and Cleveland Advertiser* of 22 October of that year:

> *We were glad to see that reference was made last week in the Town Council to the subject of a People's Park for Middlesbrough. We are sure that if the inhabitants of the town were appealed to in the matter, they would liberally come forward in its support. The want is felt by all classes in the town. No place is so badly provided for in the recreative department as ours. Sickly-looking youth and pallid manhood would receive a boon indeed by the establishment of some recreative institution or the enclosure of some ground where cramped limbs might be exercised, and the mind be dragged from the everlasting monotony around us. The lobes of the lungs are nowhere so severely tested as here and it is paramount opinion everywhere that we live in the smokiest, unhealthiest hole in the kingdom. Of course we have improved our position, and are daily improving it, but there still needs much attention – much work is yet to be done.*

Into the year 1860, the Council considered the possibility of establishing a People's Park on the site of the old brickyard pond on Linthorpe Road and it is interesting to see how Members' opinions varied as to the need for trees, some feeling that they would take up valuable open space which was needed for recreation and exercise. The question of finance was also a cause of serious concern and the matter was not resolved. It was actually from within the ranks of the earlier-mentioned Middlesbrough Temperance Society that a positive approach to a different concept was to spring – that of a privately-sponsored public park.

A Gentleman's Parkland

On 13 August 1861, the Temperance Society held its first gala day at Marton, in the splendid setting of the grounds of Marton Hall, the handsome residence which had been erected some half-dozen years earlier by Henry William Ferdinand Bolckow. A large number of townsfolk had wended their way south to enjoy the country air and a picnic, which was followed by a public meeting. During the course of the proceedings, as subsequently reported in the *Middlesbrough Weekly News and Cleveland Advertiser* of 17 August 1861, Charles Bell, the Secretary of the Society, gave a vote of thanks to Mr Bolckow for his hospitality. The following paragraph is particularly relevant:

> *And whilst seeing the people enjoy themselves in this beautiful park he could not but reflect what a glorious thing it would be if the toiling masses of Middlesbrough had a park of their own into which they might turn after the labours of the day, and if Mr Bolckow and other gentlemen would take the initiative they would not only immortalize their names, but would confer an immense public boon.*

Marton Hall, the residence of Henry Bolckow, in whose grounds the Middlesbrough Temperance Society summer galas were held. Teesside Archives Department

There is clearly no knowing if Charles Bell's remarks were premeditated or spontaneous, but they did draw a significant response from the Temperance Society's highly-respected host:

> *He was not a teetotaller himself, but he was nearly one, and highly approved of the principles. We had far too much drinking and drunkenness, and if anything could be done to stop it it was worthy of the approbation of all good men.*

It is tempting to assert that Charles Bell must have sown the Park's seed in Henry Bolckow's mind, but it is just as possible that he may already have given some thought to the matter, which had clearly been of topical interest for the past two years. What we do know, however, is that, on descending from the platform where he had been speaking, Mr Bolckow made a personal comment to Charles Bell. This was recorded in the centenary brochure of Middlesbrough Temperance Society:

> *Well, Mr Bell, your remarks about a park were good and to the point and I shall certainly consider the matter.*

An On-going Council Debate

Whatever the source of the seed may have been, Henry Bolckow nurtured it carefully and it germinated, taking seven years to the month to bear fruit. In the meantime, the subject of a People's Park was still on the minds of members of the Borough Council. It was, however, made clear that many of the ratepayers of the town were against the idea simply because of its financial implications. On 2 May 1862, some nine months after the Temperance Society gala, the Editor of the *Stockton Gazette and Middlesbrough Times* wrote strongly supporting the provision of a park in Middlesbrough:

> *Why should not Middlesbrough, then, have its 'People's Park'? Why are the thousands of her population compelled to leave home in order to enjoy a breath of pure air or a few hours pleasure? Hardly a field is there in the neighbourhood in*

which you can wander without trespassing, nor a walk in any direction where in the dry weather you are not blinded with dust or, in the wet weather, up to the ankles in mud; and even the little plantation on the south-west side of the town, that might be converted into a pleasant retreat of shady walks during the summer season, is locked up, and for aught we know to the contrary, set with steel traps and spring guns.

The writer was clearly convinced that a park was a necessity and that it would be of great benefit to the townspeople in terms of their health, recreation and moral welfare, as well as providing a meeting place for members of all social classes. He ended his column thus:

The effect of such places where they have already been established has so far been to draw the working man from the pothouse and the casino, and to give him a taste for more wholesome pleasures. We hope that the difficulties which have hitherto stood in the way of a People's Park for the smoke-dried denizens of Middlesbrough are fast disappearing, and ere long the Town Council will take up the question once more and agitate it to favourable issue.

This hope was only partially fulfilled, in that the question of a People's Park was considered once again in the following year, 1863, when the Owners of the Middlesbrough Estate offered an area of land for the purpose of establishing one. This consisted of twenty acres, including the Long Plantation, to the west of Linthorpe Road, but the Town Council felt that the financial implications of the offer were not acceptable and doubted that a park was really needed. In simple terms, they did not want to add another long-term burden to their commitments in relation to the public rates.

Henry Bolckow's Gift

Even though Henry Bolckow had not been a member of the Town Council since 1856, he must have been well aware of progress (or lack of it) in relation to the question of a People's Park, and it was in the year 1864 that he actually came forward with a formal offer in this respect. At the Council Meeting held on 13 December, the Mayor, Frank Atkinson, read out the following statement, as reported in the *Middlesbrough Weekly News and Cleveland Advertiser* of 16 December:

On Thursday, the 8th inst, H W F Bolckow, Esq, requested Aldermen Wilson and Thompson, and Councillors Bottomley, Brentnall and Buckney, together with the Mayor, to meet him in the Council Room, when he stated it was his intention to present a piece of land to the borough, to be converted into a public park for the inhabitants, working classes, &c, of the town, subject to certain conditions hereafter to be settled between the Corporation and himself. That he had agreed to purchase from Mrs Ann Walker about 92 acres of land in the Linthorpe Road, opposite to the cemetery; but as this lady, being a tenant for life, could only sell to the Corporation acting as the Local Board of Health under the powers of the Public Health Act, 1848, it was necessary that the Corporation should enter into the agreement of purchase; and he had therefore to request authority from the Council in their name to enter into the contract with her, he simultaneously covenanting by

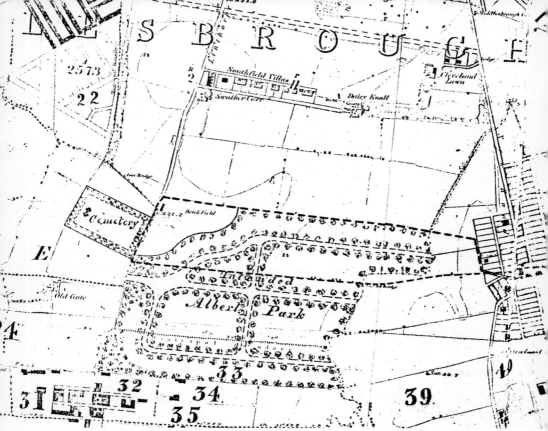

The site of the proposed Albert Park, superimposed on the Ordnance Survey map of 1856. Notice the Middlesbrough Cemetery to the north-west of the site. Middlesbrough Reference Library

formal document to hold the Corporation harmless in every respect. He further requested the appointment of a committee , consisting of the six gentlemen who met him, to make the needful arrangements with him.

This factual report in the news columns was augmented by a long and florid editorial comment on the liberality of the donor, from which the following is extracted:

The great test of liberality is considerateness, and we think this quality is eminently shown in the presentation which Mr Bolckow is about to make to the town. It is devoid of all traces of Quixoticism, for it supplies a want that is acknowledged by all. It is politic, because of all gifts that could have been imagined this will confer the greatest happiness of the greatest number of the inhabitants. We have only to look at the position of our town and the nature of the avocations which its inhabitants follow, to realise the great good that will result from a public park being available for our use. We are, as it were, shut out from all pleasant natural prospects, and the situation of the town, the nature of our field walks, and the character of the surrounding locality, is such to necessitate the exercise of little courage on the part of the inhabitant who wishes to walk to enjoy the fresh air. A park kept nice and trim, properly set off with trees and artificial waters, with suitably arranged walks and bye-ways, is just the thing to tempt the jaded artizan and the man of business out for a stroll of an evening after the confinement and harrass of the day.

Almost a year later, at a meeting of the Town Council held on 7 November 1865, consideration was given to an Agreement which had been drawn up with Henry Bolckow in order to confirm the terms of his offer to provide the purchase money for the land to be laid out as a park. At that time the land involved straddled the boundary between Middlesbrough and Linthorpe and it was necessary to approach Parliament for an Act giving permission to extend the area of the Borough southward so that the total area of the Park came within the re-aligned Borough boundaries.

The Agreement itself was embodied, as the Third Schedule, in the resultant *Middlesbrough Extension and Improvement Act*, 1866. In this lengthy document, Henry Bolckow is aptly described as 'having a local Interest in the said Borough and being desirous to promote the Comfort and Enjoyment of the Inhabitants thereof'. By the terms of the Act, he was to be regarded for his lifetime as the *Protector of the Park* and to be appointed as a member of the Committee which was required to be established in order to manage the Park itself. This Committee was obliged to formulate a series of bye-laws for the management of the Park, together with specific penalties in the case of their infringement by members of the public while visiting the Park. These bye-laws were actually issued immediately prior to the official opening of the park two years later and will be considered later.

The Town Council, as recipients of Henry Bolckow's generous gift, was obliged to acknowledge a whole series of *Stipulations and Agreements*, which were also embodied in the 1866 Act, as a Schedule to the Agreement itself. This is, in fact, a fairly hefty list, but it is of fundamental significance, as it gives us a fascinating insight into the underlying philosophy upon which the Park itself was to be established. In the legalistic terminology of the following listing, the Town Council is referred to as the *Local Board*:

- *The public Park, when duly formed and completed, shall be called by the Name of 'The Albert Park'.*

- *The Park shall be open to the Public during the whole Year upon every Day of the Week (including Sunday).*

- *The hours of opening and closing the Entrance Gates shall vary with the Season of the Year, but such Gates shall never be opened before Six o'Clock in the Morning, nor permitted to remain open after Sunset, but such Gate shall be opened as soon after Six o'Clock as the Sun rises at those Seasons of the Year when the Sun does not rise before that Hour.*

- *The Park shall only be used by the Public as and for a Promenade, and for riding and driving in such Carriages as the Local board may from Time to Time fix and determine, except that the Local Board and their Successors shall and may from Time to Time appropriate portions thereof for Cricket, Bowls, and other like Games, under such Regulations as they shall think proper.*

- *No Person or Persons shall be allowed to bathe in the ornamental Waters or Lakes of the Park.*

- *Subject to such Regulations as the Local Board and their Successors shall from Time to Time think proper to make, Bands of Music shall be allowed to play in the said Park.*

- *No intoxicating Beverages of any Kind shall be allowed to be sold or vended within the Boundaries of the said Park by any Person or Persons whomsoever.*

- *No Buildings shall be erected in the said Park except such Summer Houses, Pavilions, Lodges, or Structures of like Nature as to the Local Board or their successors may from Time to Time seem necessary or proper for the Convenience of those frequenting and using the said Park, or for the residence of the Keepers or Servants to be employed in the Care of the said Park, and except such Buildings as may be erected under the Powers and for the Purposes herein expressed.*

- *The said Park shall on no Occasion be used for the Purposes of political or any other Meetings, nor for open air preaching.*

- *The Entrance to the said Park shall be free from any Payment or Entrance Money whatsoever, and no Payment shall in any wise or under any Pretence whatsoever be taken, nor shall the said Park be in any wise used or employed for the pecuniary Benefit of any private Person or Persons, or for any municipal or corporate Body whatsoever, except in connection with any industrial or other Exhibition or Entertainment sanctioned by the Local board and the donor or his Representative for the Time being.*

- *The Local Board and their successors shall from Time to Time make and enforce such Byelaws and Regulations as to them shall seem fit for the Exclusion of improper Persons from the said Park, and for protecting and preserving from Injury the Buildings, Terraces, Statues, Trees, Lakes, Bridges, Shrubs, Walks, Gates, Fences, and Palings, and the said Park generally from Injury, with Power from Time to Time to alter or revoke any such Byelaws and Regulations, and impose reasonable Penalties for Breach of the same.*

- *The Local Board and their successors shall be at liberty to cause Boards with Notices to be put up at the Entrances of the said Park containing the Byelaws or Regulations for the Use of the said Park, and for the Exclusion therefrom of any improper Character or Person.*

- *The Local Board and their successors shall in every Year from and after the First day of July which will be the Year of our Lord One thousand eight hundred and sixty-six, or from and after such other Day as the Local Board and the Donor may mutually agree upon as the Date for opening the said Park, expend out of the General District Rate the Sum of five hundred Pounds Sterling at the least in maintaining the Buildings, Bridges, Statues, Trees, Shrubs, Walks, Seats, Fences, Waters, and Fountains in a proper and sufficient State of Repair, Order, Cleanliness, and Renewal, and for such Purposes, and for the general Purposes of the said Park, and in making needful Additions thereto and Improvements therein, and in providing, maintaining, and paying a sufficient Staff of Gardeners, Servants, and Keepers, and in the meantime, and until the said First Day of July One thousand eight hundred and sixty-six, or such other Date as aforesaid, the Donor shall and will pay and satisfy all the Expenses of maintaining the said Buildings, Statues, Trees, Shrubs, Walks, Seats, Fences, Waters, and Fountains, in a proper and sufficient State of Repair, Order, Cleanliness, and*

Renewal, and also find, provide, maintain, and pay a sufficient and adequate Staff of Gardeners, Servants, and Keepers in the said Park.

- *The annual Sum of Five hundred Pounds to be expended by the Local Board shall be made a perpetual Charge on the General District Rate of the Borough, and shall be raised and applied by the Local Board accordingly.*

The Donor: Henry William Ferdinand Bolckow

As we have already seen, Henry Bolckow was a highly esteemed local personality and it is well worth taking a brief glance at his background. The son of a country gentleman at Sulten, in the North German Duchy of Mecklenberg, he was born in the year 1806. After a partnership in the Newcastle-based general commission house of Christian Alhusen and Company, he had acquired a fortune of some £50,000 and looked out for an investment opportunity.

In Newcastle, through the happy coincidence of courting sisters, he happened to meet up with John Vaughan, the son of a Welsh ironworker, who was born in Worcester in 1799. The two men discovered that they had other interests in common

Henry Bolckow, photographed in 1868 to commemorate the official opening of the Park by Prince Arthur. Teesside Archives Department

and discussed plans for establishing ironworks in the area of the river Tees. Their intention was to settle at Stockton, but Joseph Pease, on behalf of the Owners of the Middlesbrough Estate, went to see them in 1839 and persuaded them to opt for a riverside site at Middlesbrough. The town's link with Henry Bolckow was thus established.

The rolling mill of Bolckow-Vaughan's Middlesbrough Ironworks came on line in August 1841, just a month after Henry Bolckow himself had taken up office as one of the first twelve Commissioners to be elected under the powers of the *Middlesbrough Improvement Act*. He was further honoured in local government terms in 1853, when he was elected by his peers as the first Mayor of Middlesbrough after the town had received its Royal Charter of Incorporation as a Municipal Borough. In the same year, Bolckow purchased the Marton Estate from the Rev James A Park, later erecting Marton Hall on the site of Marton Lodge, which had been destroyed by fire. In 1868, the high esteem in which he was held by the populace at large was shown when he was elected as Middlesbrough's first Member of Parliament.

The Conveyance of the Park Lands

A year before this honour was bestowed, on 23 January to be precise, a Deed of Conveyance was drawn up whereby the Corporation of Middlesbrough, in its capacity as the Local Board of Health for the Borough, formally acquired the lands on which the park was already being laid out. The document itself was actually laid before a special meeting of the Town Council on 18 February 1867, showing that the total area of land involved in the transaction was ninety-nine acres three roods and eleven perches.

The total area of land involved in Henry Bolckow's gift of the Park. In view of the key references to colours, it should be pointed out that the eight-acre site is the north-west corner, while the twenty-one acres are made up of the strips north, west and south of the park itself. Author's Collection

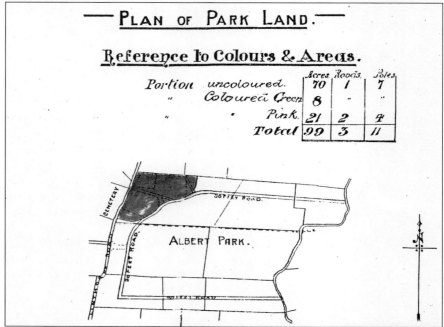

By the terms of an Indenture dated 20 March 1867, drawn up between Henry Bolckow and the Mayor, Alderman and Burgesses of the Borough of Middlesbrough, the land in question was to be divided into three smaller areas: seventy acres one rood and seven perches for the Park; eight acres for a proposed extension to the Middlesbrough Cemetery on Linthorpe Road and twenty-one acres two roods and four perches on which Bolckow intended that villas were to be built. The eight acres ear-marked for the Cemetery extension had been acquired from a Mrs Walker, who later parted with the remaining acreage after her re-marriage as Mrs Oughtred. Of the total purchase price of £19,600, Bolckow was to reimburse the Corporation by £15,000 for the Park land and £3,000 for the villa sites. By the time that he had also financed the laying-out of the Park, the total value of his gift to the town was to rise to £30,000.

Henry Bolckow's outlay of £18,000 left a balance of £1,600 to be paid by the Corporation for the remaining eight-acre proposed cemetery site, but it was never, in fact used for that purpose. It was later developed for building purposes and is now occupied by halls of residence for students of the University of Teesside. This has had the unfortunate effect of driving a developed wedge between the green areas of the Old Cemetery site (now Ayresome Gardens) and Albert Park.

In reserving for his own use the peripheral area of twenty-one acres, Bolckow was following the example of earlier park founders and he appears to have had two aims in mind. The proposed villa development was intended to recoup the cost of his benevolence, but it did not work out in that respect, as it had, in fact, for others. He also wished to have good quality building on these sites, so that there was no scope for the erection of public houses or beerhouses. In the latter respect, and, we may assume, to the great satisfaction of the teetotallers of Middlesbrough, his objective was achieved.

Research undertaken by Linda Polley has revealed that by 1868 four three-storey semi-detached villas had been erected, as Park Villas, in Park Road North. The architect was William Lofthouse and the properties, two of which were reserved for Bolckow himself, had an impressive outlook on to the Park itself. By 1875, two further villas, Hilda House and Bon Accord Lodge, had been erected, on the Linthorpe Road frontage of the Park.

The Designer of the Park: William Barratt

There can be no doubt that Henry Bolckow deserved all the praise which was showered upon him for his benevolence and foresight in providing a park for Middlesbrough, but it is equally clear that it needed a man of skill and practical experience to make the vision into a reality. The responsibility for designing the park and for supervising its physical creation was vested in William Barratt, a landscape gardener who was the proprietor of commercial nurseries and gardens situated in the St John's area of Wakefield, in the West Riding of Yorkshire. The site of the business had been conveyed to his father, John Barratt, in 1796 and in the local trades directory of 1822 the latter is listed under 'Fruiterers, gardeners, nursery and seedsman'. After his death later in that decade, the business was taken over by his sons, William and Thomas.

In 1833, William Barratt opened Subscription Botanic Gardens on the St John's Gardens site, subscribers being entitled to purchase exotic plants and seeds, as well as visiting the actual gardens. Some of the land was subsequently sold off for building development and the 'St John's Botanic Garden estate' itself was put up for sale in 1867, by which time William Barratt himself was half-way through the laying-out of Albert Park. It is worth noting that this was not the first such scheme which he had undertaken, for in 1846 he had laid out the Woolsorters' Baths and Pleasure Gardens in Bradford. The decisive step of 1867 would suggest that he was determined to pursue this line of activity as his principal interest.

Given the relevance of William Barratt's philosophy relating to the land and its management in its impact on the development of the Albert Park site, it is interesting to read something of this in his own words. On 5 April 1849, he read a paper to The Wakefield Farmers' Club with the title, *'An Inquiry as to the Best Mode of Improving and Renovating Old Permanent Pastures',* and this was printed in Wakefield in 1850. The following enlightening paragraphs have been gleaned from the introduction and conclusion to his text:

> *The man who is uninterested in the fertility of the earth, is a man either of a narrow and debased intellect, or of a selfish and ungenerous disposition. Not only is the human species dependent upon the cultivation of the soil for pleasures and luxuries, but also for 'food and raiment' and so absolutely is this the case that the arts of cultivation and the human race are found to be co-eval and commensurate, they rise or fall, flourish or decay together. We need not therefore be surprised, that in an age like ours when the spirit of change and improvement has seized upon government, upon commerce, upon mechanical arts, upon almost all the institutions and habits of men, that agriculture and its kindred occupations have shared to some extent the general changes.*
>
> *We may be forgiven for adding that with skill, industry, and sobriety combined, the soil of England yet admits of a cultivation the world cannot surpass...The earth is yet grateful, and the man who labours to produce its fruits guided by knowledge, and sustained by industry, shall not labour in vain!...The cultivator of the soil, true to the soil he cultivates, and true to himself, can no more be degraded. His green pastures and his fields 'white to the harvest,' are a true California to him – they bring him as much GOLD as he needs, and security and liberty to boot.*

On 15 February 1866, William Barratt was present in the Park on the occasion of what the Press described as 'the first gala' in the new park, which was a ceremony of tree-planting. In responding to a toast to his health, he was quoted as follows in the *Middlesbrough Weekly News and Cleveland Advertiser* of 16 February 1866:

> *Mr Barratt then shewed the influence that the park would be likely to exert on the inhabitants of the town in a moral and physical point of view, and shewed the great moralising influence that gardening exercised upon the character. Works of art, however beautiful, were only the work of men; the trees and flowers were the work of God.*

The latter statement was applauded by his listeners and it is clearly significant. William Barratt obviously appreciated the fact that his own involvement in creating the Park was only a minor part of the whole natural process. He also demonstrated his belief that the value of a park was moral as well as physical – that it was uplifting as well as recreational.

The Design of the Park

There does not appear to be an extant document which gives a specific description of the original design concept for the Park, the earliest plan being that prepared for the official opening ceremony in August 1868, to which the name of John Dunning, Middlesbrough Council's Surveyor, is also affixed. It is, however, possible to gain an impression of the design from the physical evidence and from the descriptions and opinions of newspaper commentators. At the outset, it is worth emphasising that the overall shape of the site would have been enhanced by the retention of that eight-acre segment in the north-west corner which, in the 1865 Agreement, had been earmarked as an extension to the Cemetery opposite.

In terms of its actual situation, the Park was clearly intended to provide an environment the nature of which was to be far removed from that in which its local visitors lived and worked. Even so, there would be no total evasion of the atmosphere of industry, especially if the wind came from the north. The Park was, nevertheless, well out in the country as far as the townies were concerned and that was more than good enough for them.

The principal features of the Park were intended to highlight the beauties of Nature, with a wide-ranging selection of flowers, plants, shrubs and trees. The aesthetic value of sheets of water was clearly appreciated, the two original lakes and third additional one being noteworthy aspects of the man-made landscape. Their aesthetic significance was enhanced by the introduction of fish and the presence of wildfowl and their attractions could be appreciated from bankside seats. Hills were created from which could be enjoyed magnificent views of the Park itself and the whole region around it, while the Sunk or Swiss Walk would give both shade and shelter.

Given its impressive acreage, it was possible at the outset to think in terms of a grand lay-out, with principal walkways running east-west and north-south. There was ample space for the creation of intricate and intimate walks for those in search of peaceful and restful seclusion, while those who were bent on strenuous physical exercise were presented with a choice of recreational activities, the scope of which was to increase over time.

The Victorians were noted for their love of artistic artefacts and there was an intention to have an area of statuary on a central mound where the four principal walks converged. It is not known whether this original design concept was deliberately abandoned, or if it was simply that the earmarked site proved to be the most suitable when Joseph Pease offered to present a fountain for the Park. One impressive original man-made design feature which has survived is the flight of stone steps leading from the east end of the east-west walk down to the Lower Lake.

From the extant descriptions of the Park which have been gleaned from the local Press covering the period 1868-1883, it is evident that the writers were delighted by the appearance of the Park in overall terms, but they were not afraid to comment on what they regarded as design shortcomings. For example, the slag-based landscaping of the Exhibition Ground did not find favour with all-comers and it was felt that provision should have been made at the outset for such physical needs as refreshment rooms and shelters. It can be deduced that little thought had been given to the interests of children in terms of recreational facilities, the first actual provision being that of swings in 1897. Indeed, it was a firmly-upheld ruling that the grass in

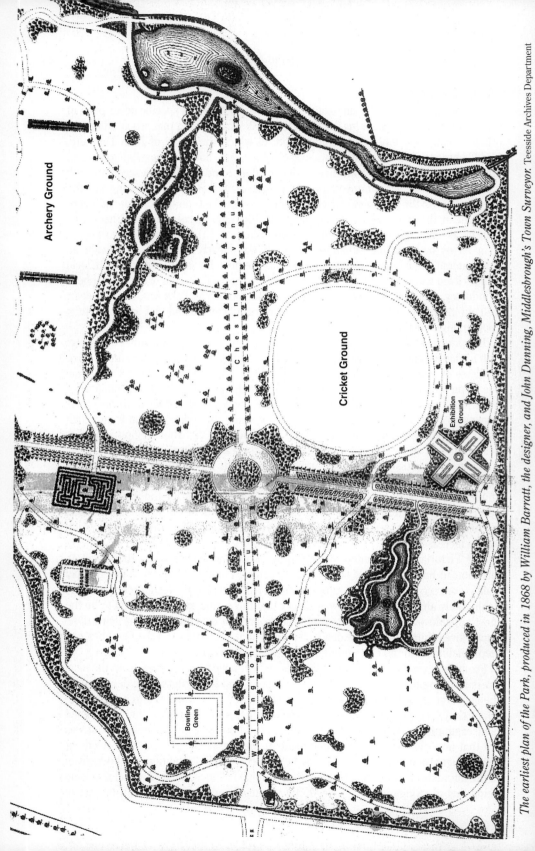

Archery Ground

Cricket Ground

Exhibition Ground

Chestnut Avenue

Wellington Avenue

Bowling Green

The earliest plan of the Park, produced in 1868 by William Barratt, the designer, and John Dunning, Middlesbrough's Town Surveyor. Teesside Archives Department

A recent aerial view of the Park, taken from the north-west. Bottom right are the University of Teesside Halls of Residence. The tennis courts, bowling greens and pavilion may be seen in the north-west sector; the children's play area in the north-east and the lake to the east. The roller skating rink is in the south-east sector and the Park Depot in the south-west. The fountain is outstanding in the centre. Courtesy of Tansee Cartwright

many areas was out of bounds. We will consider all of these elements later, within
their respective geographical contexts.

The Albert Park Design in Context

Within the general context of William Barratt's philosophy and the assessment of his
design from the physical evidence within the Park itself, the question needs to be
asked as to whether he was self-taught as a designer; whether he believed in Divine
inspiration for his work; or whether, perhaps, he was directly influenced by the work
of others involved in the designing of parks.

The fact of the matter is that Albert Park was one of many parks which came into
being in the early-to-mid-Victorian era. As we saw earlier, Middlesbrough Town
Council was debating the question of establishing a *People's Park* in the late 1850s
and early 1860's, and it is worthy of note that more than one of the parks established
at this time was actually given that precise name. In view of the huge industrial
developments taking place in Northern England at this time, it is not surprising to
discover that the great majority of the new parks were established in that region.

The first urban park in the country was commenced in 1844 at Birkenhead,
Sheffield following suit in 1847 and Bradford in 1850. The *People's Parks* at Halifax
and Hull date from 1857 and 1863 respectively, with Oldham's Alexandra Park
following in 1865. Mowbray Park in Sunderland was opened in July 1866 and
Liverpool acquired three parks in the late 1860s, while others at Manchester and
Southport date from 1868.

Some of these parks were established by local authorities, funded and maintained
by the municipal rates, while others were the gifts of men of substance who were
associated with the town and most probably owed their financial success to its
workers. It is interesting to consider whether such philanthropists (including our
own Henry Bolckow) were showing their gratitude in that respect or, perhaps,
attempting to alleviate the hardships of daily life which had been imposed upon the
town by their own industrial establishments.

The park at Birkenhead was designed by Sir Joseph Paxton, who must be
regarded as the original guiding light in urban park design. His concepts were
adopted by those who either worked directly with him or came to see his work and
gained inspiration from it. Virtually all of the Albert Park design features are
identifiable in other parks: the lakes, hills and islands (clearly inter-linked in their
construction); the lodges, ornamental gates, walkways, band stands, bridges, broad
flights of steps, gymnasia, games areas, and so on.

As far as the physical creation of a park was concerned, the designer would
sometimes entrust this task to a supervisor, who then became the Curator or Keeper.
Thus it was with William Barratt and Edward Cleaton in Middlesbrough. Paxton himself
had borrowed from earlier designers the concept of villa-building in association with a
park, not always simply on the perimeter, but sometimes within its actual boundaries. In
at least one case, the sale of building plots was so successful that it covered the cost of
the park land itself. Other parks had the further advantage of not only statuary but also
public buildings within their boundaries. Albert Park may well have been almost
unique in its maze, but Paxton had incorporated one in his design concept for the
setting of the Crystal Palace in London, created for the Great Exhibition of 1851.

Some of those involved in the designing and construction of public parks were also literary men who published their philosophies in either journals or books, thus making them readily available to others. William Barratt was obviously of the same frame of mind and it can reasonably be assumed that he would have been aware of the writings of others.

Edward Kemp was trained at Chatsworth and worked for Paxton as superintendent of the work at Birkenhead. He set up in practice on his own and went on to publish three editions of his book, *How to Lay Out a Garden: A General Guide in Choosing, Forming, or Improving an Estate*. In effect, an estate, being the acreage associated with the private residence of the noble or upper class family, may be regarded as parkland. The last edition of Kemp's work appeared in 1864, only two years before William Barratt undertook his work at Middlesbrough. The author never committed himself to a statement of his concept of an urban park, but it has been said that it would have been very similar to that of C H J Smith of Edinburgh, whose *Parks and Pleasure Grounds* had been published in 1852:

> *..it may be conceded that the city park should be more ornate, and may contain a greater multiplicity of showy objects, than would be altogether suitable in the country. It may be presumed, too, that the average taste of those who frequent suburban parks (we refer more particularly to the working classes) is not highly cultivated and severe and consequently the expression of these localities need not be so quiet, nor the style so strictly in harmony with the character of the ground, as may be deemed necessary in the secluded retreats of men of much cultivation and refinement. The public park should be gay, though not glaring or obtrusively showy. Accordingly, we would admit into it a variety of terraces, statues, monuments, and water in all its forms of fountain, pond, and lake, wherever these can be introduced without violent and manifest incongruity.*

Given that William Barratt may well have been versed in such writings, he must also have approached his Middlesbrough project in more practical terms and there can be little doubt that he would wish to see for himself the parks of noted designers. For a Wakefield man, what could have been more convenient than to visit Paxton's park at Halifax?

Presented to the town by Sir Francis Crossley, the People's Park was opened in August 1857, an event which was recorded in the *Illustrated London News* on the 22nd. The report opened with a very apt statement relating to the park movement and its social significance:

> *One of the most popular social changes of the present day is the extension of the recreation of the people by means of parks, hitherto mostly portions of private domains, and appropriated to individual possession, and the enjoyment of the royal, the noble, and the wealthy. The good old town of Halifax has just acquired a park of the former description, for the health and fruition of industrious population.*

The report presents an interesting pen-portrait of the Park itself and it is not difficult to imagine William Barratt highlighting these major features in notebook and on sketch pad during a personal visit. At this point, it is worth bearing in mind the fact that any park up to forty acres in extent was regarded as small, in the region of sixty acres being large. To the *Illustrated London News* once again:

> *The park is situated at the upper or east end of the town. Its area is twelve acres and a half. It is bounded on all sides by high mounds or embankments, protected in turn by massive lines of palisades. It has four gateways, one at each corner. Assuming the visitor enters by one of the upper gates, he will find himself after a minute's walk on an elevated piece of table-land, known as the great terrace or promenade, running directly north and south, and is attained by three flights of steps on the south and one on the north side. To the rear of the promenade stands a handsome retiring saloon, built of polished stone, and roofed with glass and iron. Placed on pedestals, ranged along the edge of the promenade, are six pieces of statuary – Diana, Apollo, Belvidere, Hercules, Aristides, Venus arising from bath, and Canova's Dancing Girl. These are from the hand of Mr. George Biennaine, Italy. Leading from the promenade to the grounds beneath is a flight of nine steps, each 27 feet in length. From this point the eye takes in at one sweep acres of rich land 'dressed in living green', winding walks, seats, bubbling waterfalls, creeping shrubs, beds of flowers, tossing fountains, curving lakes – all shut in by huge mounds, rich in vegetation, and crested with noble trees. Traversing a walk leading from the great promenade, the stroller comes upon a large stone basin, having an inside 72 feet in diameter, and holding three feet of water. In the centre a nest of fountains throw up with a prodigal hand dense volumes of water. A twelve feet walk encircles this basin, and, converging at the lower side, threads off to the bottom of the grounds. After the chief terrace and the fountains, the attention is claimed by a beautiful serpentine lake on the east side of the park. The water is supplied by pipes laid underground from the fountains. The surface of the lake covers about half an acre of land; the average depth is three feet. It is crossed by two broad bridges one constructed of rocks. Its lower margin is skirted by the eastern embankment, and fringed with ling and heather. Quitting the lake and continuing progress by the south side of the park, through dainty walks hedged in by flower-beds, grass plots, and mounds, we pass a charming summer-house, with a roof of coloured slate; and eventually reach the point whence we started – the promenade.*

On seeing the comparative compactness of Paxton's park at Halifax, William Barratt must have revelled in the development of the wide-ranging seventy-acre site at Middlesbrough and it seems clear that he took much of his inspiration from the master. It is also possible that Barratt would have visited another park with the Paxton influence, which was the Mowbray Park in Sunderland. This was opened in July 1866, when Barratt himself was based in Middlesbrough. James Lindsay was the designer of the park at Sunderland and it was actually laid out by Mr Lawson. He was gardener to Lord Londonderry, and his assistant, Joseph Smith, had worked at Chatsworth, where Paxton had been head gardener from 1826.

In simple terms, it can be stated that the Albert Park design may be regarded as typical of the period within which it was conceived.

The Inauguration and Naming of the Park

In February 1866, two ceremonies took place to formalise the commencement of the laying-out of Albert Park. Reference was made earlier to the second event, in the context of William Barratt's design philosophy, and the first ceremony actually took place on the 8th. The *Middlesbrough Weekly News and Cleveland Advertiser* of the following day recorded the fact that Mr Bolckow and an invited group of some twenty ladies and gentlemen had been involved in planting trees of the Wellingtonia Gigantea species. This activity had commenced at a point some 150 yards from Linthorpe Lane, on each side of the twenty-four-foot wide curved drive which began at the south-east corner of the Cemetery and entered the park itself at the main gate.

After the conclusion of the tree-planting ceremony, the Town Clerk of Middlesbrough, John Shields Peacock, brought to the attention of the small private gathering the question of the naming of the Park. Henry Bolckow himself had modestly declined to have his own name associated with it, which I feel was highly commendable, but equally regrettable, since it has meant that, to this day, very few Middlesbrough residents know who actually gave us the Park. I recently proved this point to myself when speaking to a local group on the subject of the Park. There was a gathering of a dozen or so in the audience and, when asked point-blank, not one of them associated Albert Park with the name of Henry Bolckow.

Referring to recent correspondence between himself, on behalf of Mr Bolckow, and Sir C B Phipps, Private Secretary to Her Majesty Queen Victoria, on the subject of a name for the Park, John Peacock pointed out that he had drawn attention to the fact that Mr Bolckow was a Prussian by birth, and that it was his wish to name the Park after his fellow countryman Prince Albert of Saxe Coburg Gotha, the late Prince Consort. The following reply was quoted to the assembled gathering:

Osborne, Jan. 20th, 1866.

Sir – I have had the honour to lay before Her Majesty the Queen your letter of the 17th inst.

I have received Her Majesty's commands to inform you in reply that she willingly gives her sanction to the Park about to be formed at Middlesbrough, by Mr Bolckow, being called the 'Albert Park'.

I have the honour to be, Sir,
Your most obedient, humble servant,
C B PHIPPS.

John S Peacock, Esq.,
Town Clerk, Middlesbrough.

In responding to eulogistic words of thanks from the Town Clerk, Henry Bolckow has left to us his personal sentiments relating to the need for the Park, with an early indication of its facilities and the timescale of its laying-out:

Mr BOLCKOW, in returning thanks, said the day was a most happy one for him. He had pondered for years the question of providing the people of Middlesbrough with the means of enjoying out-door recreation and amusement. It was most desirable that out-door recreation should be

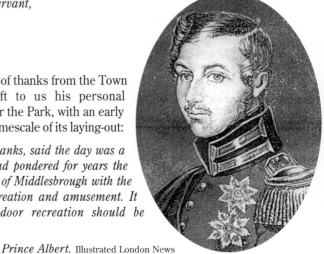

Prince Albert. Illustrated London News

provided, and nothing could give him more pleasure than to see the working man, after his hours of toil were over, taking his family to the open park, there to enjoy the scenery and breathe the pure air of heaven. He wished the park to be perfectly free and open to all classes alike, and he trusted it might be a blessing especially to the poorer classes who had not such means of recreation as the rich. He might say in conclusion that the laying out would be pushed on so that the park might be partly available for use in early summer. There would be a cricket ground, bowling green, croquet ground, archery ground, and gymnasium set aside, all of which would, he had no doubt, be of benefit, and he hoped once more that the park would prove a blessing to the town.

For over 130 years, generations of Middlesbrough residents have shared in the fulfilment of this latter hope and, as I have a habit of saying, it is to be regretted that Henry Bolckow's name is not automatically associated with his Park.

The Work of Laying-out the Park

A design concept for a particular site is no more than an idea until it is put into effect. The description of Albert Park at the time of its official opening, which appeared in the *Middlesbrough & Stockton Gazette* of 14 August 1868, gives a very interesting indication of the problems associated with the actual preparation of the site, the work involved in the laying-out of the park and the individuals responsible for specific aspects of that work. The majority of it was carried out by local contractors in Middlesbrough and Stockton, while others were brought in from Halifax and York. To read this account is to appreciate the simple fact that the park was the product of an extensive and labour-intensive exercise, which had extended over a period of more than two years:

The total length of walks in the park is about four miles; no adequate calculation can be made of the extent of the drainage, the pipes in some parts being only nine feet apart. At the commencement of the park it was feared it could never be got dry enough to walk upon, but that great difficulty has been overcome. The foundation of the whole of the walks is slag, an immense quantity of which has been brought into the park – upon a railway constructed for the purpose – and broken by a steam crusher, kindly supplied by the Middlesbrough Owners. The arduous work of laying out the park has been going on for above two years; at one time more than 150 men were employed, so that the cost for labour alone must have been very heavy. The plans for the park were supplied by Mr William Barratt, landscape gardener, Wakefield; the whole work has been carried out under his instructions by Mr E Cleeton, curator, of whom Mr Barratt speaks in the highest terms. Mr Freeman, clerk of the works for Mr Bolckow's schools at Middlesbrough, designed the walls for the entrance gates, and superintended their erection. The woodwork required has been prepared by Mr Dent, Dock Street, Middlesbrough; the brickwork by Mr John Stainsby, of Middlesbrough; the stonework and steps by Mr Joseph Lord, of Middlesbrough; a portion of the wire and iron fencing by Mr S T Stephenson, of Stockton and Middlesbrough; the iron gates and a portion of the fencing by Mr Walker, of York; the asphalting by Mr Thomas Crampton, of Halifax; and the seats by Mr Dent and Mr Blakiston, of Middlesbrough. The whole of the work has been

The signature of Edward Cleaton, the park's first Curator, taken from the Park Committee Minutes of 10 April 1869. Teesside Archives Department

executed in a most satisfactory manner, and the trees and plants in the park are in first-class condition, but the unusually dry season has of course affected for the present the appearance of the grass and flowers, which, however, are remarkably green when all the influences they have had to contend against are taken into account. Nearly the whole of the trees, shrubs, creepers, and plants were from Mr Barratt's nurseries at Wakefield, and form a fine collection.

Those of you with a keen eye for detail may have noticed the reference here to Mr *Cleeton*, compared with my earlier Edward *Cleaton*, the latter being the spelling which he himself used in his signature. William Barratt was not the only one to speak highly of him in relation to his work of laying-out the Park, a fine tribute being paid to him at the time of his resignation in 1888. This was actually brought to my attention by his great-grandson, Mr Ray *Cleeton*, of Ripon in North Yorkshire, who supplied me with a copy of an anonymous article from the *Middlesbrough Daily Gazette* of 25 May 1888. The author writes with authority and it is frustrating that we do not know who he was, or what his position had been. Perhaps he was just an interested local resident who took the trouble to monitor developments and collect interesting data. His remarks are well worth reading in their entirety, as they contain details and insights which have not been noted elsewhere:

THE MIDDLESBROUGH PARK AND ITS LATE CURATOR
(BY AN OLD RATEPAYER)

The public of Middlesbrough and many in the vicinity have just lost a valuable official, Mr E Cleeton, the late park curator, and it will no doubt be a pleasure to many of your readers to have some little record of what was done by him.

The Middlesbrough Park, consisting of 74 acres of land, was, as everyone knows, presented by the late H W F Bolckow, Esq., MP, and I trust that we and all who come after us will ever feel grateful to the latter for his most magnificent gift. The Park was, to begin with, but a waste howling wilderness, but Mr Bolckow spared no expense in making it into a paradise, the practical part of which devolved on Mr Cleeton, who laid out the ground to the best possible advantage.

What a boon the Park is to us all can be easily seen by daily frequenters. Street Arabs, nursemaids and their children, young men and their young ladies, old men and invalids, all may be seen enjoying themselves, breathing the pure air, or tripping over the flowery meads, engaged in boating, fishing, and many other kinds of pleasure. Many are the happy scenes that can be witnessed of children romping on the green sward, others gathering buttercups and daisies enough to gladden the hearts of most people who have hearts; but there are other enjoyments, not the least being the well-trimmed borders, the unrivalled flower beds, the beautiful trees of different hues and shades, &c., results of great care and skill on the part of Mr Cleeton.

On March 10th, 1866, he began his labour of love without map or plan. The task was to convert a large area of 'clay, clay, clay' into a garden of pleasure without the aid of Darwinian fertilisers. During the autumn of 1866 and the spring of 1867 there were no fewer than 165 men employed. There being no foreman appointed over these men, Mr Cleeton had to sit up night after night to prepare plans and map out work for next day's operations.

Mr Bolckow took a keen interest in all that was going on, and kept himself well posted up in every detail by summoning Mr Cleeton to his mansion every Saturday morning at 8 o'clock. It was not until August, 1868, that the Park was handed over to the Corporation of Middlesbrough, and Mr Cleeton, of course, was transferred with it to his new employers. The curator having mentioned that the Corporation would probably require some testimonial of his fitness for the post he held, Mr Bolckow said, 'Tell them to go to the Park, and see what you have done'.

No one can expect a perfect park all at once. In the absence of any greenhouses it was quite impossible to rear bedding plants for such extensive grounds, but Mr Cleeton was equal to the occasion. He sent out, far and wide, to his many friends and acquaintances, and secured over 17,000 plants, free of cost, which enabled him to make a little show in the place, but when greenhouses were erected plants were then provided by thousands, resulting in a display second to none in England, considering the soil, climate, and locality. We have sometimes heard little grumbling at the cost to the town, but all admit that through Mr Cleeton's sound management and economy the Park has been in good order for 20 per cent less than the cost of other parks and this has been ascertained by the Council only recently.

Mr Cleeton never urged his own demands very much. For some time he only received 25s per week. It was understood that he was to have £100 a year when the Corporation took over the Park, but he only began to receive this sum five years ago, after working seventeen years, so that his salary for the 22 years he spent altogether was not too extravagant, particularly when we consider that his abilities have not been confined to the Park alone. He had also to plant and decorate the New Cemetery, the Fever hospital, the Workhouse grounds, the trees in the various parts of the town belonging to the Corporation. Even the kitchen garden of the Industrial School was cultivated under Mr Cleeton's supervision for a time.

Botany and landscape were his pet subjects, and many have profited by seeking his advice, as Mr Cleeton was open at all times to give information to those who would ask for it.

In conclusion, I would ask – Are we going to allow an old and faithful servant of so long standing to leave us without giving his many friends an opportunity of testifying in some practical manner as to the excellent way he has served us?

The writer obviously hoped that something would be done to memorialise Edward Cleaton, and in that he was to be disappointed. While remembering him in the dedication of this volume, I also feel each of us can bear him in mind as, together, we later walk round that Park which he carved out of the 'waste howling wilderness'.

The Official Opening of the Park

We saw earlier that, in February 1866, Henry Bolckow had expressed the hope that the Park would be accessible to the public later that year. There is also a hint in the *Stipulations and Agreements* listed in the *Middlesbrough Extension and Improvement Act* of that year that 1 July may have been a target date, but I have not been able to confirm whether this hope was, in fact, realised. However, a description of the Park which was published in *White's Middlesbrough Directory* of the following year indicates that it was well advanced by then:

> The ALBERT PARK comprises nearly 72 acres of land, tastefully laid out and planted in 1866, and is the munificent gift of H W F Bolckow, Esq., to the borough of Middlesbrough as a place of recreation for the inhabitants. It is on the Linthorpe road, about one mile from the centre of the town, and contains a fine avenue of Wellingtonias planted by Mr Bolckow and his friends, the members of the corporation, the borough officers, &c. A handsome lake has been formed at one end of the park, and a bowling green and a cricket ground have also been provided. A circular plot in the centre is reserved for statuary; and on three sides of the park land is reserved for villas of approved design, in front of which is a macadamised road for carriages.

His Royal Highness Prince Arthur, the eighteen-year-old son of Queen Victoria, who opened Albert Park on 11 August 1868, in honour of his late father, the Prince Consort.
Teesside Archives Department

For some two years prior to the formal opening of the Park, there was considerable local interest, expressed through the columns of the Press, as to who would officiate at the actual ceremony. There was a groundswell of public opinion in favour of a member of the Royal Family and great satisfaction when it was announced that the honours were to be performed by His Royal Highness Prince Arthur, at eighteen years of age the youngest son of Queen Victoria. It was his first public engagement and represented only the second Royal Visit to Middlesbrough, the first having been by his great uncle, the Duke of Sussex, in October 1838.

Prince Arthur arrived in Middlesbrough on 10 August 1868 and was an overnight guest of Henry Bolckow at Marton Hall. On the 11th, the town was in a festive

Henry Bolckow reads his address to Prince Arthur on the occasion of the official opening of the Park. Teesside Archives Department

mood and the Park itself was decked out from end to end with flags and bunting. Dignitaries processed to the specially erected dais, where prayers were led by the Archbishop of York and speeches were delivered by Henry Bolckow and the Royal visitor, who acquitted himself extremely well on his public debut. These speeches were recorded soon after the event by Hugh Gilzean-Reid in his publication: *Middlesbrough and its Institutions: With a Record of the Opening of the Albert Park by HRH Prince Arthur*. To read the words in conjunction with the photographic record of the ceremony is to be there in the crowd of eager onlookers. Once again, we are able to gain an insight into Henry Bolckow's philosophy on the function of the Park from his own words, together with his acknowledgement, as was also the case with William Barratt, of Divine assistance in the project:

Mr Bolckow then read the following address:

To His Royal Highness Prince Arthur
May it please your Royal Highness,
I approach your Royal Highness with deep respect for the purpose of expressing through you to Her Most Gracious Majesty the Queen, my dutiful acknowledgements for having deputed your Royal Highness to dedicate to the public use of the inhabitants of this town, the park in which we are now assembled, and which it has pleased the Almighty to enable me to present to my fellow-townsmen for the purpose of healthful recreation and exercise.

Being a native of the same country as His Royal Highness, the late Prince Consort, your illustrious father, and whose watchful care of the interests of the poorer classes justly endeared him to all ranks of Her Majesty's subjects, I was naturally desirous that Her Majesty should allow this park to be named 'The Albert Park', in memory of the late Prince Consort; and this permission Her Majesty most graciously granted.

I therefore humbly request that your Royal Highness, in exercise of the authority conferred on you by Her Majesty, will now open the 'Albert Park' for the public use of the inhabitants of this Borough, and I earnestly pray that it may conduce alike to their enjoyment and to their moral and social advancement.

Dated this 11th day of August, 1868.
H W F Bolckow

The Prince accepted the address from his host and handed it to his aide, Lieut.-Colonel Elphinstone, from whom he received in exchange his own response, which he read out in a 'slow, clear, and deliberate manner':

Mr Bolckow, – I am very grateful to the Queen, my dear mother, for allowing me to represent her in the ceremony which we are now assembled to perform. To dedicate to the public use the Park which your munificence has provided would of itself have been to me a most interesting duty. On the present occasion, it has for me a far deeper and peculiar meaning.

This Park, which I am sure will contribute largely to the pleasure and happiness of the people of Middlesbrough, is to be for ever associated with the name of my beloved father, and this thoughtful mark of respect to his memory on an occasion when an act of public benefit is concerned, has truly pleased and touched my dear mother.

No one could take a deeper interest than he did in whatever ministered to the good and benefit of the people, and I feel sure therefore, Mr Bolckow, that the noble gift which you have made to this town would have been regarded by him, as I am commanded to say it is by the Queen, my dear mother, with the warmest sympathy and approbation.

Most sincerely do I join with you in praying that this park may fulfill (sic) *all the objects for which it is designed, and my best wishes do I add that you, yourself, may long live to witness the pleasure you have been the means of bestowing upon the people of Middlesbrough.*

It is not surprising to read that this address was followed by several rounds of enthusiastic cheers from the crowd of onlookers, and I am sure that if you and I had been there among them our cheers would have drowned out the rest.

The opening ceremony received the attentions of the local, regional and national Press and it was evident to all that its importance to the town would be remembered for many a long year. The significance both of the Park itself and the event of its opening was acknowledged in *The Newcastle Daily Chronicle* of 11 August as 'this epoch in the social history of the town'.

The *Middlesbrough & Stockton Gazette* of the 14th carried the following very apt statement:

> *It is unnecessary to enlarge on the benefits that this spacious place of recreation will confer on the toiling masses of this great and growing industrial community. When work is done, or on certain days of the week before it is begun, the working men now have the privilege of going out with their wives and children to breathe the balmy air and gather fresh strength amidst flowers, and grass, in their own Park – none daring to make them afraid. Well may the people be grateful for this unspeakable boon, the realisation of which they are now enjoying.*

Beyond all the pomp and ceremony, the events of 11 August touched the lives of local individuals in their own situations and the memories of two of them allow us to have fascinating little glimpses behind the scenes. One of these was a boy of seven at the time and he later recorded the event in his diary as an adult. George Herbert Metcalf was born in Middlesbrough in 1861 and had family connections with the village of Old Linthorpe, where they had occupied a cottage near the Blue Hall. In 1884, he wrote:

> *I can remember Mr Hodgson taking us children to the top of the Blue Hall and also into his joiner's shop to let us look towards the Albert Park to see the soldiers as Prince Arthur was going to open the Park.*

At 8.30 that morning, Prince Arthur, accompanied by Henry Bolckow and a number of dignitaries, had visited the Eston Mines, from which the firm of Bolckow-Vaughan had been extracting ironstone since 1850. The Mines Manager was Thomas Lee, who recorded that particular visit in his journal. He also noted as follows:

> *The morning had been fine up to this time but rain began to fall and continued to do so at intervals heavily during the day which very much spoiled the proceedings in opening the Park at Middlesbro.*
>
> *I attended the Banquet at the Exchange in the evening at which was the Prince & Party, they leaving about 10 to attend a Ball at Mr Bolckow's.*
>
> *The Town was beautifully illuminated and hung with flags and some grand fireworks were exhibited on the waste ground adjacent to the railway Station.*

The First Park Bye-Laws

In May and June 1868, the Council's General Purposes Committee considered the question of drawing up a series of bye-laws for the management of the Park and Henry Bolckow was invited to join a Sub-committee for this purpose. The Town Clerk having taken advice from other authorities already involved in the management of parks, a series of twelve bye-laws was published on 8 August 1868, just three days before the official opening of the Park. Listed below, they are well worth comparing directly with the *Stipulations and Agreements* on page 21:

1. Every person (except the officers and servants of the Local Board) shall leave the Park by the time the bell, which is rung for fifteen minutes before the time of closing the same, has ceased to ring, which time for closing shall be stated on a board fixed at the main entrance to the Park.

2. Every person who in the Park shall conduct himself in a disorderly manner, or shall be intoxicated, or guilty of gambling, or shall use any improper or indecent language, or shall offer to sell any refreshment except as authorised, or shall take any dog into the Park, or if a male shall intrude on or use any playground or place set apart for the use of females, or if a female shall intrude on or use any playground or place set apart for the use of males, or shall without the sanction of the Council take any vehicle or horse into the Park, or shall destroy or injure any building, terrace, rockery, statue, lake, fountain, bridge, walk, seat, gate, fence, paling, tree, shrub, plant, or flower, or pluck any flower or leaves, or shall take or disturb the nest of any bird, or shall obstruct, hinder or prevent any officer or servant of the Local Board in the execution of his duty, or who, on Sunday, shall play at any game, shall for each and every such offence be liable to a penalty not exceeding the penalty hereinafter mentioned.

3. No person shall walk on the grass of the Park excepting where the same is set apart for public amusements.

4. No person shall take or destroy or attempt to take or destroy any fish in any of the ornamental waters, lakes or streams of the Park, without the permission in writing of the Park Committee first had and obtained.

5. No person or persons shall bathe in the ornamental waters, lakes, or streams of the Park.

6. No bands of music or musical instruments shall be allowed to play in the said Park without the consent in writing of the Park Committee having been previously obtained.

7. No intoxicating beverages of any kind shall be sold or vended within the boundaries of the said Park by any person or persons whomsoever.

8. No building shall be erected in the said Park, except such summer houses, pavilions, lodges, or structures of a like nature as to the Local Board or their successors may from time seem (sic) necessary or proper for the convenience of those frequenting and using the said Park, or for the residence of the keepers or servants to be employed in the care of the said Park, and except such buildings as may be erected under the powers and for the purposes herein expressed.

9. The said Park shall on no occasion be used for the purpose of political or for any other meetings, nor for open-air preaching.

10. The entrance to the said Park shall be free from any payment or entrance money whatsoever, and no payment shall in any wise or under any pretence whatsoever be taken, nor shall the said Park be in any wise used or employed for the pecuniary benefit of any private person or persons, or for any municipal or corporate body whatsoever, except in connection with any industrial or other exhibition or entertainment sanctioned by the Local Board and the donor or his representative for the time being.

11. Any officer or servant of the Local Board may exclude any person from the Park who is offensively dirty or indecently clad, and may also remove therefrom any person who shall be guilty of any breach of the Bye-Laws for the time being in force or any part thereof.

12. THE PENALTIES for every breach or non-observance of any and every part of the foregoing Bye-Laws shall be any sum not exceeding five pounds, and the Justices before whom any penalty enforced by these Bye-Laws is sought to be recovered may order the whole or part only of such penalty to be paid, or may remit the whole penalty.

The Management of the Park

From the beginning, and as required by *Act of Parliament*, the actual management of the Park was placed in the hands of the Park Committee, with full responsibility for the supervision of day-to-day matters and long-term planning. Edward Cleaton was the first Curator, in the early days also occasionally referred to as the Park Keeper. He, and his successors, lived in the West Lodge, situated at the main entrance to the Park, and he was directly responsible to the Committee, reporting to them at each meeting in relation to progress and problems. Park security was in his hands and his men took it in turns to ring the warning bell in order to clear the grounds prior to the locking of the gates at sunset. He always had to be aware of infringements of the above bye-laws and submitted regular reports on offences committed within the Park.

The first Curator tendered his resignation to the Committee on 24 April 1888 and there were fifty-nine applicants to be his successor. Charles Anderson was appointed on 14 May 1888 and his death was reported to Committee on 22 January 1895. There were forty-three applicants for the vacant post and Henry Rymer was appointed on 8 February 1895. He died in December 1922 and was succeeded by his son Samuel, the Park Foreman, who had already overseen the daily running of the Park during his father's illness.

The first reference to the curatorial post as being that of Superintendent occurs in the Committee Minutes of 8 April 1930 and Samuel Rymer's retirement due to ill-health was reported on 19 March 1943. Seven applicants were interviewed for the post and Harry Courtenay Hildyard was appointed, taking up his duties on 1 July. It was he who vacated the West Lodge as his residence and he moved to the newly-acquired house at 40 Croydon Road. Five years later, in the spring of 1948, he moved to a cottage at Stewart Park, this, the town's second park, having been opened twenty years earlier. The post of Deputy Parks Superintendent had been created in 1942, first held by J W Gott, promoted from Foreman, and his successor, J S Harper, took up residence at 40 Croydon Road after Harry Hildyard's departure from there.

Considerable length of service was a common feature in the careers of the early

Park managers and it is interesting to note the occurrence of promotion from within the Department. Another significant factor which is evident in the Minutes is that the Committee clearly placed great store on the advice and suggestions of the Curator and, later, the Superintendent. He was the man on the spot, with his finger on the pulse of the Park, and his opinion mattered. It was also clear to the Park Committee that there was one area of management in particular where it had to rely heavily on the support of another Committee. That area was the maintenance of public order and it was the Watch Committee to which it turned for direct help from the Chief Constable and his officers.

A regular Police presence was requested for the Park and it is interesting to note that in the early days PC Morrison actually lived in one of the two cottages associated with the East Lodge and PC Hogg occupied the other. In April 1896, the Park Committee suggested that plain clothes officers should be on patrol, then it was felt that a change of faces would be another way of outwitting offenders. From 1884, the Park Committee had agitated for a number of their own employees to be sworn in as Special Constables, but it was not until 27 November 1906 that six of the workmen took on this additional responsibility in terms of protecting the Park from offenders. Given that it was always intended to be a haven for recreation and relaxation, it was clearly felt to be of crucial importance that visitors should be able to regard it as a place of safety.

My analysis of the Parks Committee Minutes has revealed the following offences, as reported to Members by the Curator or Superintendent:

Assault	Killing duck
Bad language	Murder
Bird-nesting	Playing football
Burglary	Plucking flowers
Bye-laws infringements	Poaching fish
Catapult-firing	Rape
Damage	Ringing Park bell
Disorderly conduct	Rowdiness
Dog control faults	Spitting
Exposure	Suicide (and attempted)
Fishing	Theft
Indecent conduct	

The most common offences were associated with vandalism, whether to property or flora, but it can be seen that the above list, which is well worth comparing with the original bye-laws, as detailed on page 41, is a mixture of both minor and extremely serious misdemeanours.

The Park Workforce
It is very easy to give all the credit to management for the efficient running and maintenance of the Park, but I believe that good chiefs reflect the hard work of good braves. In this respect, it is very satisfying to have some awareness of the Park's original workforce.

At the meeting held on 27 August 1868, the Park Committee agreed that the workforce to be employed in the Park should consist of the following eight men, at the weekly wages indicated:

W Campbell	18 shillings	L Cleaton	10 shillings
W Addison	18 shillings	A Cleaton	6 shillings
W Lawrence	18 shillings	I Starke	6 shillings
I Gill, Jnr	16 shillings	M ?	6 shillings

This, then, was the original team which, under the day-to-day supervision of Edward Cleaton, was responsible for carrying out the work in the Park to the standards set by the Committee. The Minutes of their meetings reveal the pressures which this work entailed and the ways in which the Curator and his staff endeavoured to meet them.

Overtime payments became a feature of the process and additional manpower was drafted in at particularly busy periods of the season. In his reports to Committee, the Curator highlighted the routine work and major projects in hand and it is clear that the workforce was always busy, no matter what the weather conditions were like. It is possible to see how this local team kept abreast of wider trends in labour relations, whether it was the nine-hour-day movement, the forty-four-hour week, or, in due course, Trade Union affairs, and the proposed five-day week.

The men were apparently not afraid to approach the Curator with their demands and he was able to convince the Committee that additional recompense was due for such duties as cleaning privies, unlocking the gates and ringing the bell. In order to maintain constancy of work, the Curator himself suggested that lunch-hours should be staggered. It also seems that he was quite capable of cracking the whip in terms of discipline, dismissal following disobedience or bad conduct. One employee in particular, a boatman named John Hudson, was regularly in trouble because he was unwilling to undertake duties which he felt did not fall within what he saw as his area of responsibility. On 18th July 1911, he was summoned before the Park Committee and severely reprimanded by the Chairman, who ordered him to obey the Curator's instructions in future.

At the same time, however, the Curator was always prepared to speak up for the men as far as their wages were concerned and his recommendations for increases were well received by Committee Members. When manpower was needed on the occasion of public holidays, or in the event of national celebrations such as Coronations, he arranged for the men to receive extra pay. His own financial progress can also be traced through the Minutes, from being on a weekly wage to an annual salary.

Whenever they were on duty, the men were expected to be aware of what was going on in relation to the behaviour of members of the public. From 1880, steps were taken to give staff an obvious identity in terms of a uniform and arrangements were made for them to wear caps and armbands.

Over and above the increasing work-load imposed by the routine of maintenance and improvement in the Park itself, the workforce also became involved with the care of a series of recreation grounds and open spaces in various parts of the town. Furthermore, the special skills of the men became of interest to other Committees. Assistance was requested in Cemeteries, Hospital grounds, public highways, and so on, and every effort was made to comply with such requests. In times of depression, the Poor Law Guardians requested the involvement of the Park Committee in allocating work for men on their official lists and this, too, was taken on board.

With the on-going expansion of the Borough of Middlesbrough in the twentieth century in relation to suburban developments, the original Albert Park-based workforce evolved into a Parks Department with responsibility for several actual parks, the recreation and sports grounds and open spaces, roadside trees and verges, and so on. For that reason, it becomes more and more difficult to disentangle the workforce input to Albert Park in its own right.

One point of general interest is the fact that many men appear to have spent most, if not all, of their working-lives at the Park. On numerous occasions, the Curator, and later the Superintendent, was asked by a colleague to approach the Committee on his behalf in order to arrange for the extension of his service beyond the normal retirement age of sixty-five.

There is evidence to show that careers were interrupted by military service in both World Wars and that this had the effect of increasing the work-load of those colleagues who were not involved. After the cessation of hostilities, the men returned to the jobs which were still there for them. Certainly after the Second World War, however, some of them did not stay very long, having discovered that better wages were available in local steelworks and the chemical industry.

By virtue of the very physical nature of the routine work in the Park itself, the workforce was, historically, male-dominated, with only occasional references in later Committee Minutes to female employees, until the advent of a succession of clerical assistants within the context of the office.

The actual manpower of the workforce was supplemented by horsepower and Ken Sherwood, who started work at the Park in 1943 at the age of fourteen, remembers with great affection some of the fine cart horses which were based there. Sandy was an old fellow who had worked in general haulage and he had a habit of letting his tongue hang out of his mouth. Sometimes Ken would simply roll it up and pop it back in, while on other occasions Sandy would do this for himself after his tongue-end had been rubbed with a sweet.

A horse named Jimmy was bought from a farm at Carlton, Ken himself having to walk there from the bus stop in Stokesley to collect him and then being advised to walk him back to Middlesbrough because he was too young to ride. He was a nervous horse and on the cart run to the Council's coke depot in Snowdon Road, in the St Hilda's area of the town, he was terrified when going under the Albert Bridge in case it was crossed by a steam train. It was not safe to drive him by the reins because he would take the cart all over the road and Ken had to jump down in order to lead him by the head. Even then, Jimmy would rear up and dance through on two legs, which must have been quite a performance!

Beauty was the last horse to work in the Park and she, like Sandy, had a sweet tooth. Sometimes, she would be standing there on a path with her cart and her attention would be caught by a mother and child sitting on a seat with a bag of sweets. When one of these was produced for the child, Beauty would lumber across with her cart in tow and loom up over the seated pair. This was enough to frighten them, but

George Archer with Beauty, the last horse to work in the Park. Ken Sherwood Collection

Ken Sherwood poses with colleagues John Robinson and Ernie Hughes in 1983. Ken Sherwood Collection

Beauty meant no harm and was, in fact, regarded as a pet by visitors to the Park. She simply stood there until a sweet was offered and that was all that she wanted. Her working life ended in May 1969 and she was greatly missed when she had to be put to sleep.

The True Value of the Park

We have a saying that people will 'vote with their feet', and in this respect public appreciation of Albert Park was demonstrated at an early period after its opening in Edward Cleaton's report to Committee. He had the following to say on 10 April 1869:

> *I consider it my duty to state to you that the people of Middlesbrough seem to appreciate the park as the number of visitors increase daily and their conduct while in the grounds is of the most exemplary character. Last Sunday there would be about 4,000 visitors in the park and not a single case of misdemeanour or vandalism occurred and this order and good conduct was secured with the nominal superintendence of one Park Constable and Policeman which show I think that the people of Middlesbrough have a clear appreciation of Mr Bolckow's gift and Keats' saying that a thing of beauty is a joy for ever.*

It is, perhaps, a sobering thought that Edward Cleaton was impressed by the fact that there was no bad behaviour or damage in the Park to report, implying that he would not have been surprised if the opposite were the case. However, this commendation from the man on the spot would doubtless be most encouraging to Committee Members, and two years later the curator's interest in visitor statistics was picked up in a most complimentary statement in the *Middlesbrough Weekly Exchange* of 10 August 1871:

> *How the privilege of a visit to the Park is valued may be gathered from the fact that on busy days, according to the estimate of Mr CLEETON, the Park-keeper, no less than 10,000 people go thither for an outing. On Sundays the walks are alive with people, who, if the pleasure depicted on their faces be any index, regard an outing in this meadowy and bowery enclosure as the one 'treat' of the week, no other being attainable in this district of restricted railway privileges and inconsiderate railway management. The Park is, without doubt, a lung to a busy and hard-working community, and to strangers is a place well worthy of a visit.*

The true value of Henry Bolckow's gift to the people of Middlesbrough was further highlighted in the local Press a decade later, when the *Middlesbrough Daily Exchange* of 18 May 1881 had the following to say:

> *The Park is the most popular of any of our municipal institutions, and is also one of the most useful. It is a grand lung for a smoky town, and a visit to it at any time is a source of pleasure and delight to those who are during the day spent in close confined offices, or have to undergo the drudgery of daily toil in our large manufacturing establishments.*

These sentiments were further echoed by James Paling in 1898, when writing in the excellent little book, *Middlesbrough, Its History, Environs and Trade*:

Few provincial towns possess a park at once so beautiful and so admirably adapted to provide recreation for its community. To the people of Middlesbrough it is an incalculable boon, and needless to say is much frequented by all classes.

For those of us who are accustomed to the wide range of sophisticated pastimes and entertainments which are available in an age of ever-increasing technological skills, it is, perhaps, difficult to appreciate what a great boon Albert Park was for the whole community. It may be quite impossible for us to imagine a daily existence and a weekly routine in which a visit to the Park would be regarded as *the* outstanding highlight. That, however, was clearly the way in which Middlesbrough folk regarded it for many years.

With the regrettable disappearance of virtually all physical evidence of industrial sites and the loss of many original townscapes, the Park is to be treasured as symbolic of Middlesbrough's Victorian heritage. It dates from a period of explosive development and expansion, when the town itself mushroomed in order to keep pace with the riverside industries and their demands for workers. It was given by an industrialist for the benefit of the workers and their families, and they blessed him for it. For them, it provided a bolt-hole – a means of escape from the town into the rural suburbs. It gave them a sense of freedom and a means of recreation in a setting where they were able to enjoy the beauties of Nature.

The actual creation of the Park, in terms of both its design and its laying-out, was a tribute to all those who were involved in it, and in that sense it reminds us of the heritage of achievement – of high standards set and attained. In the same way, the modern citizens of Middlesbrough should appreciate the way in which every effort has been made to maintain and care for the Park by Committee, management and workforce over a period of 130 years. As times have changed, and tastes with them, its facilities have been adapted in order to maintain the tradition of providing for the recreational needs of the community.

The Park was unique in the town for almost sixty years, but the number of open spaces and smaller parks has increased in line with the on-going growth of the urban area. This, however, does not detract in any way from the fact that Albert Park still holds a unique place in local history. It has played an important part in the life of the town and touched the lives of many generations of all ages. Its original Victorian grandeur may well have faded with the passing of time, but the Park is still a haven in suburbia.

Chapter Two

The Restoration of the Park

The On-going Concept of Improvement
At various points during the course of its more recent history, plans have been introduced for the restoration and re-development of the Park's original image.

The 1984 Annual Report of the Parks Service set the scene for a number of improvement proposals:

Many people use the park not only for the recreational facilities which the Parks Service provides, but enjoy the visual and aesthetic qualities the park has to offer, the freedom from motor vehicles and noise, the attraction of the boating lake and children feeding the ducks, are all important qualities which must be preserved and enhanced.

Unfortunately, over many years Albert Park has slowly become more run-down, mainly due to shortage of manpower, financial resources and conditions which are often beyond the control of the Service, such as Dutch Elm disease and the consolidation of the ground which has led to extreme flooding.

At that time, plans were being drawn up for the following:

- The alleviation of poor drainage
- The up-grading of all facilities
- The provision of new facilities, such as an Outdoor Zoo area and a pets corner
- The improvement of the general lay-out: footpaths, mounding, ornamental lakes, etc.

These proposals were designed to 'encourage people to use the facilities and attract people back who have become disappointed with the general appearance of the park.' The Parks Service hoped to 'encourage school parties and a general resurgence of interest in Albert Park from the general public.' They believed that 'Albert Park is too valuable a resource to allow it to continue in its present situation indefinitely.'

These laudable sentiments were expressed again in 1992, when information was circulated to each household in Middlesbrough in order to outline plans for the development of the Park and to ask for feed-back in terms of public opinion. At the time, it was envisaged that it would take several years to implement all the proposals being put forward.

The two principal short-term objectives were to create an integrated play area in the north-east quadrant and to provide a new visitor/information centre, to be based at the West Lodge. The north-west quadrant was to have floodlit games courts and a new pavilion and there was to be new woodland on the south-west flank of the lake, which was, in itself, to be enhanced as a wildlife centre. The former Cricket Ground site in the south-east quadrant was ear-marked as an Events and Activity Area and the Depot site in the south-west quadrant would become a car park, with a Sculpture Walk to the west.

Redevelopment plans formulated in 1984 led to the creation of these water features to the west of the site of the Cannon Lake. Photo George Ward

As with all well-intentioned schemes, their full implementation was very much dependent upon financial resources and, consequently, progress was limited. It was, indeed, not until 1996 that circumstances presented themselves whereby serious consideration could be given to the preparation of a broadly-based Master Plan for the actual restoration of the whole Park, which was, interestingly enough, to echo several proposals from these earlier schemes.

Even when the opportunity was actually there to set about the implementation of long-held aspirations, it became clear that the process of acquiring the necessary funding was, in itself, to be a major undertaking. The simple fact is that the Albert Park Restoration Scheme took five years to evolve from an inspirational idea to actual work on the ground.

The National Lottery Heritage Fund

The Heritage Lottery Fund issued information relating to its new Urban Parks Programme and it was clear that Middlesbrough Borough Council was in a position to apply for financial support from this source. The guidelines for applicants contained the following significant paragraph:

1.1 Parks, gardens and open spaces of all kinds play a significant part in enhancing the quality of life for millions of people in the United Kingdom. Urban parks and spaces were often created in the past with this in view; many are now suffering from neglect and lack of care. The National Heritage Memorial Fund (NHMF) through the Heritage Lottery Fund offers an exciting opportunity to reverse this decline and to make a real difference to parks and open spaces throughout the United Kingdom. With lottery money, we want to encourage new ideas and to galvanise thinking about how such places can play a more fulfilling role in the life of the community around them.

Applying for Heritage Lottery Funding
Having decided to proceed with all necessary arrangements to apply for restoration funding, the Council had to undertake a feasibility study for the project. The Heritage Lottery Fund made provision for subsidising this initial project and their general philosophy in the Urban Parks Programme was indicated in their guidelines for applicants:

Applicants are expected to provide evidence of the following:

- *heritage importance of the land, buildings or collections which will be the object of the study*
- *likely heritage benefits of project*
- *likely public benefits of project*
- *that all reasonable preliminary studies have been undertaken from within the applicant's own resources*
- *the study is essential to the ultimate quality of the project and cannot reasonably be met from other sources*
- *around 25% of the cost of the study will be met by the applicant*

The Selection and Appointment of Consultants
In the Summer of 1996, I myself became involved in the proceedings, with a view to being appointed as researcher and compiler of a historical/heritage report, as an essential element within the Master Plan, which was to be prepared by consultants. My appointment was confirmed on 8 October, so that my work could be undertaken before the actual process of selecting and appointing consultants was set in motion.

The Council prepared a Brief for the guidance of those who wished to apply for appointment to undertake the task of producing the Master Plan, and it was clearly stated that it was the heritage aspects of the Park which were to be emphasised. There were five distinct objectives to be used as the basis of the document for submission to the Heritage Lottery Fund:

- *To build on the existing historic fabric in order to ensure that the criteria are met for a successful bid to the Heritage Lottery Fund.*
- *To improve and diversify the leisure facilities of the Park based on the established needs of the local and wider community which it serves.*
- *To ensure a good relationship between the Park and adjacent facilities, such as the Dorman Museum and Clairville Stadium/Common and integrate the area as a key leisure corridor within the Borough.*
- *To stimulate community spirit and interest through public involvement in the development and management of the Park.*
- *To ensure that any proposals represent value for money, will be capable of phased implementation and of being supported mainly through the Heritage Lottery Fund.*

It was necessary to embody these objectives within the framework of practical guidelines for the content of the submission document and they were presented to the consultants in the form of seven major principles:

- *Research into the history and development of the Park, including historic maps, archaeological records, published articles and pictures, photographs, aerial photographs and ecological surveys. The historical investigation shall be carried out by the Council's nominated Consultant, Norman Moorsom.*
- *A site survey to identify and describe the existing and historic landscape features, built forms and planting, including topographical survey. A tree survey has been carried out for the Park and the information will be available from Middlesbrough Borough Council.*
- *An analysis of the various changes which have taken place over the history of the Park.*
- *An analysis of the current management practice and funding.*
- *Investigation of the current role of the Park within the environmental, social, economic, and other corporate strategies at local and town-wide level. Socio-economic data for the catchment area will be available from Middlesbrough Borough Council.*
- *Investigation of the current usage of the Park (Visitor Surveys and Focus Groups with Non-Visitors).*
- *Research into and identification of additional sources of funding which may be available for capital projects.*

Based upon the findings of their surveys, the consultants would be required to produce within their Master Plan the following costed elements:

- *A Development Plan, outlining general proposals for the Park with specific reference to Heritage related aspects based upon an analysis of survey work.*
- *A Management Plan, outlining proposals for the future management of the Park taking into account those aspects covered by the Leisure Management Contract, the Albert Park Consultative Committee and on-site management. This should involve proposals for continuing involvement during the construction and future management of the Park.*
- *A Business Plan to assess the financial implications of proposals in terms of both revenue and capital costs, over the next 20 years.*

Within the Consultant's Brief, the Council indicated the timetable to which it intended to work. Consultants were to submit their tenders by 24 January 1997 and shortlisting would be completed by the 28th, with the selection of the successful applicant. In due course, Landscape Design Associates of Peterborough were actually appointed to undertake the work.

The Consultants and the Heritage Lottery Fund Submissions

Once the work was in hand, it was closely monitored by the above-mentioned Albert Park Consultative Committee, which was made up of elected councillors, residents and groups who regularly used the Park. Particular attention was paid to the involvement of Community Councils which operated in the immediate vicinity of the Park. They were fully briefed on plans and developments and were given the opportunity of having a factual presentation of the Restoration Project at one of their meetings.

Between 25 August and 13 September 1997, a survey was carried out in the Park in order to glean opinions and attitudes from both regular and less frequent visitors. The survey took place at key times of day and each fieldwork session lasted for three-and-a-half hours. Each of the thirty-one sessions involved two interviewers, giving a total of 217 hours of dialogue.

More than half of those interviewed were in the Park in the school holidays, while nearly half were present between the hours of 12.30 p.m. and 4.00 p.m., the vast majority being young people who went into the Park on several days each week. Nearly half of those approached were in family groups, while others were either alone or with a dog. Reasons for being in the Park included going for a walk or looking at the scenery; bringing their children to the play area, or to see or feed the ducks; walking the dog, or simply taking a short cut.

With regard to features and amenities in the Park, opinion was generally favourable in relation to gates, memorials, sports courts and bowling greens, the children's play area, floral arrangements and trees, but people were generally disappointed with the toilets, refreshment facilities, signposting and information, boating facilities, water features, litter bins and car parking facilities. The historic feature most favourably mentioned was the sun dial, while the lodges were generally regarded as being of the least importance. The vast majority said that they would be interested in information on the history of the Park if it were made available in the Park.

The interviewers enquired about any feeling of being at risk in the Park and those visitors who acknowledged that they did feel unsafe stated that it was because of drinking, drug use and a lack of security. A minority admitted that they actually felt unsafe in the Park because of a personal bad experience. On a more positive note, however, it was found that there was general satisfaction with the management of the Park in terms of staff presence and helpfulness.

Finally, those interviewed were asked for any further comments or suggestions about the Park, most of which elaborated on the themes of security and safety. It was also pointed out that there was room for improvement in relation to facilities for visitors with special needs, with particular reference to toilet facilities.

In addition to this exercise of actually meeting Park users head-on on site, all residents living within some 500 metres of the Park were circulated with an Albert Park Consultation leaflet, with the opportunity of passing on their opinions by means of a response form. In conjunction with the data gathered on site, all information gathered in this way was of great assistance in helping the planners to balance supply with demand. There was regular Press publicity as their plans evolved, while exhibitions, displays and presentations were staged at numerous venues in the town.

Given the preponderance of youngsters within the total number of those who regularly visited the Park, links were established with local schools: Abingdon Road Junior, St Joseph's, Linthorpe and Sacred Heart Primary. An opportunity was given to them for direct involvement in the restoration planning process, by means of a 'Play Watch' exercise. Nearly a hundred pupils took part in the workshop, being told about the history of the Park and having the opportunity of helping to draw up plans for its future development. They were also asked to produce models to illustrated their ideas and these were displayed in the Park Pavilion.

There is no evidence to even suggest that public opinion about the original planning of the Park was ever sought in 1866, nor, it may safely be assumed, would the public expect any such involvement. As we have seen, however, local residents did follow the evolution of the Park plans with great interest and occasionally had something to say about them in the local Press. The simple fact was that they could not fail to be delighted by the uniqueness of the Bolckow gift of a 'People's Park'. Well over a century later, however, it was seen as an essential part of the restoration planning process that the people themselves, of all age groups, should be positively encouraged to have their say.

The official launch of the Albert Park Restoration Project was undertaken by the Mayor of Middlesbrough, Councillor Oliver Johnson, at the Dorman Museum on 30 October 1997. The highlight of the evening was an illustrated presentation by Tim Marshall, Director of the highly successful restoration of Central Park in New York. Based upon his own experience in the field, he was able to emphasise the main elements involved in the process upon which Middlesbrough was then embarking.

I always enjoy a personal involvement in an event which I regard as being history in the making and duly went along to this function at the Museum. The occasion was subsequently recorded in my diary:

I was given my lapel name badge and went up to the reception area, where there were drinks and nibbles. I chatted to a number of people in there, then at 7.30 p.m. we were ushered through to the new gallery. I picked up a leaflet on the Albert Park Restoration Project and there were opening addresses by Geoff Rivers, Chief Officer of Community Development, Libraries and Leisure, then Councillor Oliver Johnson, Mayor of Middlesbrough. He then introduced Tim Marshall, an American involved in the revitalisation of Central Park in New York. He gave a slide presentation on the work involved in that project and it proved to be very interesting. That Park is over 800 acres in extent and the funding is both public and private.

In February 1998, Landscape Design Associates presented a Draft Report for consideration at a meeting of the Joint Strategy and Standards Sub-Committee and the Albert Park Consultative Committee, the latter being part of the Community Development, Leisure and Libraries Committee. In the Introduction, there were some remarks which I read with great personal interest:

This present report draws on an existing document Albert Park, Middlesbrough: History and Heritage *completed by Norman Moorsom in April 1997. The 1997 Report was commissioned by Middlesbrough Borough Council in preparation for the Lottery bid and was the result of extensive archival and documentary research into the history of Albert Park. It contains a detailed account of the history of the park and its features. This present report is intended specifically to meet the requirements of the Heritage Lottery fund and to address aspects not covered by the 1997 report, such as an analysis of the historic landscape character of the park and the way the landscape character qualities have changed over time.*

Since the archival research undertaken in the preparation of the 1997 Report was wide-ranging and thorough, no further archival research has been undertaken in the presentation of the present report. The 1997 Report therefore forms the primary documentary source for this present report, supplemented by historic maps, photographs and contemporary descriptions of the park in its early years, the majority of which were reproduced in the 1997 Report. Particularly valuable were four local newspaper articles from 1868, 1871, 1881 and 1883.

It was to be just over three years from the date of the launch of the Restoration Project to its successful negotiation of the two stages involved in the formal application for approval. A Stage 1 application was submitted to the Heritage Lottery Fund in August 1998, comprising an impressive body of material assembled by the Consultants. They were required to include within their presentation a statement of their vision of the future for the Park and this embodied distinct echoes of Henry Bolckow's original thinking when first presenting the park to the citizens of Middlesbrough:

The restoration of Albert Park should re-create the quality and character of the nineteenth century Park, so that it has a strong and attractive image, as a place where people of all ages, cultures and abilities can enjoy various forms of active and passive recreation in a beautiful, well kept, caring and safe environment.

The specific aims set out as the means of making this vision into a reality were:

- *To protect, restore and re-create the design intentions of the nineteenth century Park landscape, focusing particularly on the core features relating to the axial walkways and Lower Lake.*
- *To improve and diversify opportunities for formal and informal recreation in the Park, based on the established needs of the local and wider community within the context of the history of the Park.*
- *To stimulate community spirit and encourage participation and involvement in the development, management and maintenance of the Park, developing a strong sense of local ownership and pride.*
- *To encourage greater awareness of the historical significance of the Park and promote opportunities offered by the Park for health, education and leisure purposes.*
- *To ensure that any proposals represent value for money, and will be sustained and built upon in the long term.*

Middlesbrough Borough Council was informed of the decision by the Heritage Lottery Fund to approve this application in a letter dated 20 July 1999, but attention was also drawn to the fact that further detail was required on a total of eight specific points. The process of preparing the Stage 2 Application began on 4 November 1999 with a meeting between the Consultants and officers of the Heritage Lottery Fund and, as requested, each of these highlighted matters was attended to. A further meeting took place on 2 March 2000, so that progress on formulating the second submission could be assessed, and reactions were generally favourable. It did, however, become clear that the Lottery Fund representatives wished to obtain the opinion of English Heritage in relation to specific aspects of the proposals. This body was actually to be involved in the final

A notice posted in the Park to inform members of the public about the Albert Park Restoration Project and the Heritage Lottery Fund. Photo Tansee Cartwright

assessment of the Stage 2 Submission.

In order to comply with this request, a meeting was held in the Park on 5 April with Andy Wimble of English Heritage. The design development work then under way was presented to him and a walk round the Park allowed for the consideration of specific proposals. General impressions were very favourable and constructive comments on some aspects of the development work led to a further refinement of the content of the Submission.

Another body which became directly involved at the planning stage was the Environment Agency, whose advice was sought with particular reference to various aspects of the works to be undertaken on the Lower Lake. These included fisheries, the provision of a borehole water supply and the disposal of sediment to be dredged from the lake. The possible toxicity of the latter was queried locally, but assurances were given that the sediment was safe.

In view of the fact that a major element within the second phase of the Restoration Project was to involve the Park's historic Grade II listed structures, it was essential that a survey should be carried out in order to assess their condition. This survey was undertaken by Hirst Conservation of Sleaford, Lincolnshire, whose report was finalised in May 2000, with the snappy title, *Survey work to Cast Iron Clock Tower, Sundial, South African War Memorial, Entrance Gates and Memorial Walls, Bolckow Bust and Monument on Front of West Lodge, Albert Park, Middlesbrough.* It was later

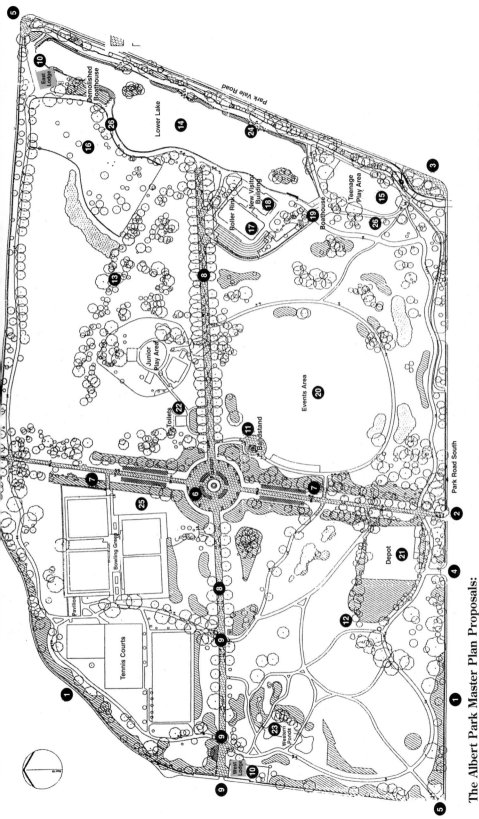

The Albert Park Master Plan Proposals:

1. Boundary planting; 2. North and South Entrances; 3. South-East Entrance; 4. Vehicular Entrance to Depot; 5. North-East and South-West Entrances; 6. Fountain and Surrounds; 7. Italian Walk; 8. East-West Walk and Steps; 9. Historic Structure; 10. West Lodge and East Lodge; 11. Bandstand; 12. Site of Upper Lake; 13. Sunk Wall; 14. Lower Lake; 15. Teenage Play Area; 16. Putting Green; 17. Roller Rink; 18. New Visitor Building; 19. Boathouse; 20. Events Area; 21. Depot; 22. Toilets; 23. Western Ponds; 24. Fishing Platform; 25. Picnic Area; 26. Lighting

estimated that the cost of this element of the Restoration Plan would be £136,600. The following paragraph in the Introduction to the Survey Report adds a nice little human touch:

> *Elizabeth Hirst and Matthew Webster, of Hirst Conservation, visited Albert Park on Wednesday, 10 May 2000. During the morning the assistant park manager (Stuart Johnston) was in attendance. A light weight two section ladder was provided for access. The weather was overcast, with fine drizzle and a north westerly light breeze. The temperature was not recorded.*

The revised Stage 2 Application was submitted in the following month, June 2000, and the final document also included an elaboration of certain aspects of the historical section, which was undertaken by Linda Polley of the University of Teesside. It was approved by the Board of Trustees of the Heritage Lottery Fund on 14 November of the same year, thus giving the official go-ahead to the Albert Park Restoration Project. In effect, this was its date of birth, after a prolonged, and somewhat involved, period of gestation.

The actual work of putting into practice the plans for restoring and developing the Park was scheduled to take place in two phases, over a period of three to four years. Phase 1 would concentrate on the eastern end of the Park, including the Lower Lake, the roller skating rink, the north-east and south-east entrances, a new Visitor Centre, a new toilet block, a new boathouse and a new teenage play area. The Phase 1 contract was let to Land Engineering, with Dorrin Construction as sub-contractor for the building works. This work began in June 2001.

Phase 2 comprises the remaining built infrastructure of the Park (depot, footpaths, railings, etc), and work of a special nature (historic features, fountain, band stand, gates, listed buildings and planting). The work was scheduled to commence in 2002 and it was envisaged that the Council's own Direct Services personnel would work in conjunction with appointed contractors.

The total cost of the Restoration Project will be £4,492,170, which can be broken down into the following funding components:

Item	Amount
Middlesbrough Borough Council Capital budget	£ 692,313
MBC revenue budget (over a five-year period)	£ 61,757
Private Sector Contribution (Northumbrian Water)	£ 73,373
Stage 1 Sunk Costs	£ 13,663
Stage 2 Sunk Costs	£ 156,937
Contributions in Kind	£ 125,000
Heritage Lottery Fund Grant (75% of £4,492,170)	£3,369,127
TOTAL FUNDING PACKAGE	£4,492 170

The sum of £125,000 noted as Contributions in Kind will be accounted for in relation to volunteer labour, one voluntary group in particular being worthy of note – The Friends of Albert Park.

Chapter Three

The Friends of Albert Park

As we saw earlier, the Albert Park Consultative Committee, consisting of elected councillors, residents and groups who regularly used the Park, was fully involved in the process of preparing the way for the restoration of the Park. At their meeting on 15 December 1997, they considered the question of extending their remit in order to act as a basis for *volunteers, or 'Friends of the Park', to participate more actively in works on the ground. They would also be able to support both the day-to-day activities of the Park and development proposals.*

Operating initially under the name of the *Albert Park Lake Group*, a small number of enthusiasts first met in the Park Pavilion in February 1998. By April of that year, they had adopted the name of *Friends of Albert Park* and were meeting in the Park's West Lodge, which was to become their permanent base. Members drew up a document embodying a formal Constitution and Rules, in which their aims and objectives were clearly stated:

- *To gather and disseminate knowledge of all aspects of the Park*
- *To seek the opinion of Park users and other interested parties*
- *To produce and distribute publicity material*
- *To formulate proposals for improvement of the Park*
- *To send representatives to meet and discuss with the Park authority*
- *To assist in the implementation of suitable schemes*
- *To raise income to cover its expenses by means of members' subscriptions*
- *To apply for and accept grants and donations in cash or kind towards its work*

At an early stage in the proceedings, and as evidence of their serious intent, a document was drawn up which highlighted members' feelings with regard to the lake and its problems, which they listed as follows:

- *Lack of healthy vegetation in and around the lake*
- *Dirty water*
- *Litter*
- *Lack of fish*
- *Lack of sheltered breeding areas for fish and fowl*
- *Imbalance in bird numbers*
- *Injury and sickness among birds*
- *Old and unsuitable boats*
- *Vandalism, especially of boats and boathouse*

The following specific objectives were listed as a means of improving the situation at the lake:
- *To improve the water quality*
- *To improve the visual appearance of the lake*

- *To encourage a greater variety of wildlife in, on and around the lake*
- *To protect and care for the wildlife in, on and around the lake*
- *To improve the facilities for the recreational use of the lake*

As we will see later, the lake was to feature prominently in the Phase One Restoration of the Park and it is well worth bearing in mind the above points in that context.

The Friends had been active for several months before the Consultative Committee recorded its formal agreement to their formation, and the activities of their first full year of operation were recorded in a report compiled by the Secretary. This sheds interesting light on the actual origins of the Friends and makes clear their genuine concerns about matters relating to the Park:

The year 1998-99 has been the first year of operation for the Friends of Albert Park. The association developed out of protests against a proposal to let the anglers manage the lake. The proposal was dropped, and the park management expressed their desire to see the formation of a body to represent park users.

In March 1998 the founder members formed themselves as a committee which has met more or less monthly since then and has met council officials regularly to discuss matters of concern about the park. Membership of the association currently stands at 33. No subscription was levied for 1998-99.

Middlesbrough Council has supported the association both financially and by the provision of facilities. In particular, the Council has allowed the Friends to use the West Lodge as its base. The Council has improved the facilities in the Lodge, and the Friends have redecorated the interior. The Lodge is open daily from 1p.m. to 4p.m. as an information centre and meeting place, and for the provision of refreshments, manned entirely by volunteers from the Friends.

The lake has been, and continues to be, a serious cause of concern, and several meetings have been held with senior managers and with engineers to discuss the problems and possible solutions. An application for NWET (Northumbrian Water Environment Trust) *for a substantial grant to undertake major improvement works on the lake was unsuccessful. Co-operation with the Council has been impeded by changes of management during the year. Earlier this year the Council abolished the Consultative Committee which was the only formal provision for public consultation on matters affecting the park, and no successor body has yet been announced.*

The Council continues to be absorbed by its application for a Heritage Lottery fund award for the restoration of Albert Park, and currently maintenance of the park suffers in consequence.

Written representations have been made to the park management on the following topics:

- *Renovation of the North Gate - our offer to repaint the gate was turned down.*
- *Vehicles in the park – our concern at the number of vehicles, official and unofficial, was 'noted'.*
- *Control of fishing - our concern at the lack of regulation of fishing in the park was 'noted'.*
- *Boating - our concern at the inadequate control of the behaviour of boaters was 'noted'.*

- *Duck tunnel - our proposal that the old play area near the fire station should be made available to the water fowl, with a duck tunnel under the path, was rejected.*
- *Computer software - our request for better software on the computer in West Lodge was rejected. (The park's computer has since been removed from West Lodge, and we have provided our own computer and suitable software).*

It should be noted that, since the writing of this report, the original Consultative Committee has been succeeded by a Consultative Group, which, although attended by fewer Council Members, maintains the public forum for the Friends and other Park users.

The Friends themselves are to be commended for their on-going, practical interest in the welfare of the Park, and for their input into the proposals for its restoration. When the latter is complete, they will have the great satisfaction of knowing that they played a significant part in the process.

Chapter Four

A Visit to the Park

I feel that the most appropriate way in which to consider the detailed proposals which were put forward by the Consultants in their Stage Two Submission Document is to link each of them directly to specific features of the Park as we embark together upon a leisurely tour of inspection. If this is actually your first visit, you will be pleased to know that there is no need for walking boots, or, for that matter, any other special gear (weather permitting, of course!).

For those of us who have been familiar with Albert Park all our lives, it may be difficult to imagine its impact on visitors at the time of its creation. It seems to be a safe assumption that members of the public would have access to it some time before its official opening in August 1868 and there can be no doubt that visitors would feel that they were entering another world. As we have seen, *An Old Ratepayer*, writing in 1888, described it as a *paradise*, and, in doing so, he was probably not exaggerating public feeling.

The majority of visitors, as was Henry Bolckow's intention, would be from the working classes, whose domestic situation was, in many respects, very basic. That is not to say that they all occupied sub-standard accommodation, but by the nature of the mushroom development of the town in mid-century, housing stock left much to be desired and areas of the original 1830s properties had degenerated into slum conditions. With the demise of the Jowsey Park in the dockland area, the only stretch of greenery in the older part of town would be that of the ancient burial ground, which had been associated with the medieval Middlesbrough monastery and subsequent agricultural community.

When attempting to imagine the initial reaction of visitors to their own new park, it may seem to be rather poetic to say that they would feel as though they were entering upon the Elysian Fields of classical mythology, reserved for the souls of the blessed, but I honestly feel that this would be pretty close to the truth. It brings to mind a report in the *Middlesbrough Weekly News and Cleveland Advertiser* of 23 July 1859 which described an organised picnic excursion to Roseberry Topping, in which it is clear that the event represented a great escape from the polluted fog of industrial Middlesbrough into the sweet air of rural Cleveland.

As we ourselves visit the Park today, we will do well to remember the work situation and home life of those who were there before us at the very beginning, an approach which will help us to appreciate more fully what Henry Bolckow's gift would mean to them.

The Main Entrance Gates and the Memorial Walls
When considering the principal design features of Albert Park, those involved in the process must have been aware of the great importance of first impressions. Possibly for that reason, the main entrance gates, on the west side facing Linthorpe Road,

The first main entrance gates to the Park, which were purchased by Henry Bolckow in 1866 from Walker's of York. Author's Collection

were of particular interest to Henry Bolckow himself and he became personally involved in their selection.

They were constructed by William Walker, at his Victoria Foundry in York, as a special exhibit at the Yorkshire Fine Arts and Industrial Exhibition, which was held in York itself in 1866. The firm of John Walker, William's father, had been established in about 1800 and specialised in producing large ornate wrought iron gates. The firm gained an international reputation and in 1847 received royal patronage, supplying ironwork for Sandringham. Great success was achieved at the Yorkshire Exhibition, where the firm was actually awarded a medal for 'elegance of design, and superiority of workmanship', as reported in the *Yorkshire Gazette* of 3 November 1866.

It is also a local newspaper which gives us an early description of the entrance gates and adjoining walls at the time of the opening of the Park in August 1868. The following is from the *Middlesbrough and Stockton Gazette* of the 14th:

The gates of the park are approached from Linthorpe Road by a carriage drive, 120 feet wide at the entrance and gradually narrowing towards the gates, which furnish a beautiful specimen of iron-work, and elicited much admiration when shown at the York Industrial Exhibition last year. They are 26 feet in width and 16 feet 6 inches high, and are flanked by massive recessed winged walls, each 50 feet in length. These walls are surmounted by ornamental vases, giving the entrance to the park a very fine and finished appearance. The iron gates and a portion of the fencing by Mr Walker, of York. Mr Freeman, clerk of the works for

Mr Bolckow's schools at Middlesbrough, designed the walls for the entrance gates, and superintended their erection.

It is to be regretted that these original gates and walls have not survived to the present time, but their removal and replacement can be ascribed to a very good cause. The following reference to the gates and associated walls appeared in the Minutes of the Park Committee after their meeting of 20 April 1922:

ENTRANCE GATES. ALBERT PARK. – The Town Clerk reported that in the scheme for the erection of the War Memorial adjoining the main entrance to the Albert Park, provision had been made for the erection of new Entrance Gates and panelled walling on which the bronze tablets containing the names of Soldiers who fell in the War would be inscribed, and it was now for the Park Committee to decide as to how the existing Gates should be utilised.

The Committee made an inspection on the site.
Ordered as follows:
1. That the Committee agree to the removal of the existing Gates and Boundary Walling at the Park Entrance, subject to no cost in connection therewith being placed upon the Park Committee.
2. That in view of the fact that the existing Gates at the Main Entrance to the Albert Park were the gift of the Donor of the Park (Mr H W F Bolckow), the Park Committee agree to their re-erection in Park Road North, immediately facing Linthorpe Road and Parliament Road, and that a new entrance into the Park be constructed for that purpose, this work also to be carried out without any cost to the Park Committee.

Within a week, the matter was given further consideration, at a Committee Meeting held on 25 April:

WAR MEMORIAL. - The question of the re-erection of the Main Entrance Gates at the Albert Park after being removed so that the New Gates which form part of the War Memorial Scheme, can be erected, was discussed.

The Mayor (Councillor J G Pallister), kindly offered, on behalf of the Mayoress and himself, to re-erect the gates at the place suggested, at their own cost, in order that the present Main Entrance Gates may be preserved as a Memorial to the late Mr H W F Bolckow, the donor of the Park.

Once the work on the War Memorial was under way, it became necessary to close the main gates to the public and the following order was issued by the Park Committee at their meeting of 10 June 1922:

That the Main Entrance to the Albert Park be closed until the Contractors for the War Memorial have completed the new Wall and Gateway, and that the Chairman, Borough Engineer and Park Curator be authorised to make an entrance to the Park opposite the Tank in Park Road North, at the place where it has been suggested the existing Entrance Gates should be re-erected, and that the Borough Engineer be authorised to carry out the necessary work.

The panelled Memorial Walls and the gate piers are of Portland stone, the wrought

The dedication of the Cenotaph on 11 November 1922, together with the Memorial Walls and the new entrance gates. Middlesbrough Reference Library

ROBINSON, JOHN W.
ROBINSON, JOSEPH
ROBINSON, JOSEPH
ROBINSON, LESLIE L.
ROBINSON, SAM¹ C.
ROBINSON, THO⁵
ROBINSON, THO⁵ E.
ROBINSON, THO⁵ E.
ROBINSON, THO⁵ W⁵
ROBINSON, WILLIAM
ROBINSON, W⁵ A.
ROBSON, ALBERT
ROBSON, JAMES
ROBSON, JOHN H⁷.
ROBSON, MARK
ROBSON, ROBERT H⁰
ROBSON, STANLEY
ROBSON, STEPHEN
ROBSON, T. O.
ROBSON, TOM R.
ROBSON, W. O.
ROCHE, JOHN
RODDY, T.
RODGERS, A.
RODGERS, FRED⁵
RODGERS, HAROLD
RODGERS, JOS. A.
RODWAY, WILLIAM H⁷
ROE, JOHN
ROGER, GEORGE A.
ROGERS, ANDREW
ROGERS, ARTHUR
ROGERS, J.
ROGERS, JAMES
ROGERS, JOHN
ROGERS, JOHN JA⁵
ROGERS, JOHN W⁵
ROGERS, JOSEPH
ROGOWSKI, ARNOLD E⁷
ROOKE, ARTHUR E.
ROONEY, EDWARD
ROPER, GEORGE
ROSE, SAMUEL
ROSKELLY, W. R.

ROUND, ENOCK
ROUTLEDGE, ALFRED
ROWDEN, ALFRED
ROWE, J.
ROWE, JOHN E.
ROWLANDS, A.
ROWLANDS, J. W.
ROWLANDS, TOM E.
ROWLANDS, W.
ROWLEY, FRED⁵ THO⁵
ROWNTREE, GEO. A¹⁰
ROYER, GEO. ARTH⁷.
ROYLE, W.
RUDD, WILLIAM A.
RUDDY, THOMAS
RUDGE, REGINALD T.
RUMENS, DOUGLAS
RUMMITT, HARRY
RUMMINGS, D. J.
RUSH, R.
RUTLEY, WILLIAM
RUTTER, J.
RUTTER, THOMAS A.
RUTTER, WILLIAM
RYDER, JAMES E.
RYDER, JOHN E.
RYDER, RICHARD R.
RYDER, ROBERT W⁵
RYLATT, ALBERT H.
RYMER, JAMES
RYMER, ROBERT
SADDINGTON, N.
SAILS, J. H.
SALMON, JOHN
SANDERS, E.
SANDERS, E. T.
SANDERSON, A.
SANDERSON, E. W⁵
SANDERSON, H⁷
SANDERSON, T. GEO.
SARGENT, S.
SAUNDERS, JA⁵ W⁵
SAUNDERS, W⁵
SAUNDERS, W⁵ H⁵

SAWER, THOMAS
SCALES, JOHN
SCALES, T.
SCALEY, G.
SCARLETT,
SCOTT, ALFRED
SCOTT, PETER
SCOTT, GEO.
SCOTT, HENRY
SCOTT, JOSEPH
SCOTT, PERCY
SCOTT, WALTER
SCREENEY,
SCREENEY,
SCRIMGOUR,
SCRUTON,
SCUFFHAM,
SCURRAGE,
SCURRAH, ALMA G.
SEAMAN, ALBERT
SEAMAN, ALFRED
SEAMAN, GEO. E.
SEAMAN, JOHN H.
SEAMAN, T.
SEAMAN, WALTER
SEARBY, FRED
SEATON, ALBERT
SEATON, JOHN
SEATON, J. H.
SEAVERS, GEORGE
SEED, GEORGE
SELBY, CHARLES W⁵
SELKIRK, WILLIAM
SERGEANT, CHARLES
SETTLE, HARRY
SHANE, T.
SHAUGHNESSY,
SHAVE, EDWARD
SHAVE, HARRY
SHAW, ABRAHAM
SHAW, FRANK
SHAW, JAMES
SHAW, JOHN
SHAW, JOHN

iron gates being fashioned by T Elsley of London. The two dozen bronze panels, listing alphabetically the names of the War dead, were the work of the Birmingham Guild Ltd. This Memorial and the handsome Cenotaph opposite were dedicated on 11 November 1922, being the fourth anniversary of Armistice Day, which brought the First World War to an end.

During the Restoration survey of May 2000, it was discovered that the lettering on the bronze panels was still in good condition, but that the surfaces were affected by corrosion in the form of copper oxides, possibly through the deterioration of the protective wax coating. There was also evidence of pitting, possibly stemming from the presence of fine sand as part of the original casting process. The Portland stone of the Memorial Walls shows evidence of bronze staining from the panels, while some areas are cracked. At a higher level, there is

One of the name tablets associated with the Memorial Walls of 1922. Photo George Ward

Pedestrian access through the main entrance gates of 1922. Middlesbrough Reference Library

evidence of a build-up of algal growth. Subsequent to their survey, Hirst Conservation recommended a detailed programme of cleaning, repairing and re-pointing the walls and of cleaning and re-waxing the memorial panels.

In 1978, it was decided that the entrance gates should be inspected after it was discovered that park gates had been the cause of a fatal accident in another part of the country. It was subsequently discovered that those in Middlesbrough were unsafe and they were removed as a precautionary measure. In the belief that they were the original Victorian gates, which, incidentally, do not appear to have actually been preserved and re-used as proposed, they were stored in the Albert Park works depot. It was, however, finally decided that it would be more cost-effective to replace

The main entrance gates of 1982. Photo George Ward

them rather than to renovate them. A team of a dozen youngsters involved in a Manpower Services Commission scheme undertook the work as a special project. The new gates were officially opened in February 1982.

As part of the Restoration Project, the existing gates are to be replaced by copies of the 1922 design, using the evidence of historical photographs and the surviving wrought iron piers. The installation of this fourth set of gates will give the present ones a lifespan of some twenty years, compared with fifty-six years each for the first and second sets.

Other Entrance Gates
The Park Committee Minutes indicate the development of access into the Park from different points on its perimeter. The north-east gate, near to which the East Lodge was subsequently erected, was first mooted on 7 January 1869, while on 29 April 1890, a new one was planned at the east end of the Park, with a footbridge over the Marton West Beck. Also at the east end, and for the convenience of those using the allotments on the Clairville Road Recreation Ground, a section of railings was converted into a gate in 1917. On 13 May 1919, it was ordered that a new entrance should be formed at the south-west corner of the Park, for the use of people approaching from New Linthorpe. During the Second World War, a barrage balloon was situated on the south side of the Park and in 1941 it was decided to provide direct access to it by means of a new entrance gate on Park Road South. More information on the latter will be found in Chapter Five.

The new gates at the south-west entrance, created in 2001. Photo Tansee Cartwright

The north gate, leading into the Italian Gardens, retains its original stone pillars and these are to be replicated in restoring the south gate. In both cases, wrought iron gates re-create the character of the originals. New gates and stone pillars have been erected for the north-east and south-west entrances. The latter gates were designed by Sue Woolhouse and constructed by steel fabricator John Hay. A group of residents from the Surestart Parenting Network on Abingdon Road was involved in workshops to cast and produce glass discs for insertion into the gates themselves.

In conjunction with the gates restoration programme, consideration is also being given to the renovation of the boundary railings and the renewal of boundary planting, all of which will improve the general setting of the Park and its initial welcome to visitors.

The Walkways and Their Trees

On actually entering the Park itself, it is interesting to consider its lay-out in relation to the basic pattern of the walkways within its boundaries. In simple terms, the whole site is quartered by its four main walkways, running from west to east and north to south, converging at the central fountain. The north-south axis, the Italian Garden, will be considered when we reach it on foot.

The walkway from the main entrance to the fountain was originally known as the Wellingtonia Avenue, while its extension from the fountain to the Lower Lake was the Chestnut Avenue. In the *Middlesbrough and Stockton Gazette* of 14 August 1868, these two major promenades were described in the following terms:

> *The centre walk, opening from the entrance gates, is 750 feet in length, and 15 feet in width, and is planted on each side with Wellingtonias - most of which are memorial trees planted by different individuals at the invitation of Mr Bolckow –*

The Wellingtonia Avenue at the time of the official opening of the Park in August 1868. The trees themselves had been planted two years earlier. Teesside Archives Department

which will, in a few years, form a beautiful avenue.

The main walk is continued from the opposite side of this promenade for a further distance of 1,000 feet, when it is terminated by a handsome flight of stone steps, leading to the lower lake. The walk is planted on each side with three varieties of horse chestnuts... .

I conjectured earlier about William Barratt, the Park designer, making a visit from his base in Wakefield to the People's Park in Halifax, and it is certainly clear that he made use of materials from that area in his work at Middlesbrough. The flight of steps noted here, and considered more closely later, was actually made from Halifax stone.

Unfortunately for posterity, the aspirations of the journalist of 1868 with regard to the 'beautiful avenue' of wellingtonia trees were misplaced. The weather conditions following their planting, were simply not conducive for them to flourish and within a few years they had failed. In 1871, indeed, the general state of all the park's trees was remarked upon by the commentator in the *Middlesbrough Weekly Exchange* of 10 August:

Of course there are many adornments which the lapse of years only can supply. The trees, except in one or two cases, are of very limited growth.

Just over a year later, on 5 December 1872, the Curator reported that twelve wellingtonia trees had been presented to the Park by C F H Bolckow, Esq, presumably in a bid to revive the flagging fortunes of the main avenue. Under the simple heading of *Avenue,* the Minutes of 6 January 1876 reveal that two additional

One of the curved and gravelled side walks of the Park in 1868, with a fine array of young visitors. Teesside Archives Department

rows of chestnuts and oaks were to be planted, under the superintendence of a nominated sub-committee. On the following day, it was ordered that these trees on the Main Avenue were to be planted in clusters 'as protection to the best trees until grown up, the inferior removed and the choice ones kept.' There is no specific reference here to wellingtonias, but great care was obviously being taken to

The Lovers' Walk, which led from the southern inner walk to the Cannon Lake. Author's Collection

The Park contains many groupings of trees, as woods or copses, and here we see perhaps the best single specimen – a Turkey oak. Photo David Kelsey

Even when a tree has been felled, its stump can nurture fine specimens of fungus. Photo David Kelsey

safeguard the appearance of the principal promenade in the Park.

The wellingtonias would normally have been expected to achieve a height of fifty feet at maturity and their demise was a sad loss. They were subsequently replaced by chestnuts. As far as the Chestnut Avenue to the east is concerned, we find an interesting anecdote in the *Middlesbrough Daily Exchange* of 18 May 1881, which adds a nice human touch to Council Members' involvement in the appearance of the Park:

> *The central lower avenue of trees leading from the fountain to the lake are doing well and present a thriving appearance. The trees in this avenue were re-planted some years ago when various members of the Park Committee pitched upon particular trees as test trees, and each selected the one which he thought most likely to grow in the park. Mr T H Bell chose the sycamore, Mr T L Dalkin the Turkey oak; Mr J Dunning the horse chestnut; Mr R Todd the elm; and Mr T Brentnall the oriental plane. Mr Todd's selection is making the most headway, and some of these trees made no less than five feet last summer. There is a tie between Mr Bell's and Mr Dunning's selection. The Turkey oak occupies a good position in the race, but the plane is very variable, in some cases doing well and in others not thriving as could be wished.*

At the time of its opening in 1868, it was estimated that the Park contained some four miles of walkways, some of the initial surfacing being gravel. Later, however, the practice of asphalting was to become more common, a point which was highlighted by 'A Rambler' in the *Middlesbrough Daily Exchange* of 6 September 1883:

> *Coming down to the east lake, I noticed that the committee have laid a new asphalte pavement from the north entrance to the promenade steps, and I understand it is in contemplation to continue the same course round the west side as far as Mr Chapman's house, and along the centre avenue that crosses the park from south to north. This, of course, will involve somewhat serious cost, and it is possible that this consideration may delay for a time the intentions of the Park Committee. Of course, if this improvement is carried out, it will make a splendid promenade for visitors, and will also be a good track for the bicyclists, who come down between six a.m. and nine a.m. to take their morning exercise.*

Cycling

Just over a year before 'A Rambler' observed these bicyclists, on 13 May 1882 to be precise, members of the North Eastern Bicycle Club were given permission by the Committee to cycle in the Park. Initially, in order to safeguard pedestrians, normal access for cyclists was between the hours of 6.00 a.m. and 9.00 a.m., the latter time being gradually extended until it reached 11.00 a.m. in 1896. After that time, cycles could not even be wheeled unridden in the Park and it was not until 1910 that this restriction was lifted. On 24 June 1884, however, the Middlesbrough Cycling Club was refused permission for evening access. It was always expected that cycles would be fitted with bells and on 26 June 1888 a speed limit of six miles per hour was imposed for both bicycles and tricycles. On 20 September 1927, it was decreed that fairy cycles and invalid carriages should be prohibited after 10.30 a.m.

Today, the Park has a section of a public cycleway within its boundaries as part of a cross-town route, but this does not involve access to the footpaths in the Park itself.

The Public and Short-cuts
Returning to the matter of footpaths, it may be noted that the Park Committee Minutes reveal that members of the public created footpaths of their own away from the main walkways, presumably simply through habit as convenient short-cuts. One of these proved to be of concern to the Curator on 24 December 1888, when he recommended that it should be stopped. It led 'from Mr. Hedley's gate, across the Cricket ground to the lower Lodge', and he was afraid that it would become an eye-sore. On the other hand, however, he was anxious to improve matters when he felt that it was necessary, as is shown in a recommendation to Committee on 26 March 1889:

> *May I ask you to allow me to open a footpath for the convenience of Ladies with Perambulators, using the Centre Walk, at present there is no other course than up and down the stairs facing the Lake. Forming a narrow walk from the top of the stairs leading into the sunk walk would do away with this inconvenience.*

In both of the above instances, the Committee agreed that the Curator's proposals should be put into effect. He, after all, was the man on the spot who had the hands-on experience to evaluate situations and to make practicable recommendations.

Over three decades later, on 20 April 1926, the Curator expressed his real concern over the serious effects which the public practice of short-cutting between the main paths was having on floral borders and areas of grass. His detailed report is well worth reading in full, as it highlights not only the nature of the problem itself but also the varying degrees of understanding and support exhibited by different sides of the legal system in attempting to solve it:

> *PARK DAMAGE AND DISFIGUREMENT*
> *Following the Committee's decision at your last meeting, I interviewed the Chief Constable on the above matter and asked him if he could assist by giving a little more police supervision in the Park, that we may endeavour to stop the constant practice of crossing on unsightly tracks over the grass, which have been made by many careless people during the last few years. A great number of these people have absolutely no respect for the place and when corrected are very indignant and impertinent, to say the least, and at certain points they cross the short mown on the ornamental flower borders regularly, the sole object being a short cut to and from main footpaths and gateways of the Park.*
> *The Chief Constable, though short handed promised to give all the help he possibly could and has had an officer on duty in the Park each day since. This policeman came in at 10.0 a.m. on the 20th ultimo. I walked around with him, pointing out and explaining the chief things requiring attention, these being crossing flower borders and tracking through plantations, bringing in dogs without a leash (which I must say is a very serious matter and should if possible be stopped), and the disorderly behaviour of certain persons visiting the Park.*

For the first week the Constable spent much of his time watching flower borders, etc., and warned many offenders that, if they continued this practice, they would be prosecuted. In the meantime, I repaired the damaged portions of the flower borders, erected fencing, dug over the tracks preparatory to sowing of grass seeds, relayed (sic) new turf on the borders near the main footpaths, and fixed notice plates near the fenced portion requesting the public not to walk on the grass in this part of the Park. Unfortunately many people still persisted in going against the regulations and of course the policeman in duty bound took their names.

A number of these offenders appeared before the magistrates on the 9th instant, the first case being that of two women for crossing a flower border, who the Constable informed me were really the worst offenders as they read the notice plate and one of them said 'We had better not cross here', the other one remarking, 'Oh yes, come along, it is sooner.' Without hearing any evidence the learned Stipendiary dismissed these cases, remarking, that whilst he understood the difficulties of the Parks Committee and the fact that repeated warnings had not had the slightest effect on previous offenders, in this matter, he felt keenly that the shame of standing in the Court dock might have been spared these ladies, by the Constable administering a simple warning, and he admonished the Watch Committee in severe terms.

With all due respect to our esteemed Stipendiary, I can hardly agree with him in his remarks, as this has become a serious matter, warnings being of no avail in very many cases, which has been proved during the past few years. Many of these offenders come through the Park regularly and know from repeated warnings alone that this kind of thing is not allowed, but seem determined to do as they like. If people persist in ignoring Notice plates and infringing the Rules, then in my opinion the only alternative is that they must be proceeded against.

The next case was that of a youth, 16 years of age, who read out the Notice plate aloud than walked on the grass. A friend who was with him told him to come off, or he would be getting into trouble, he then deliberately jumped on the Plate and the Constable seeing him, took his name. At this juncture, it was evident that the Stipendiary realised that these cases were more serious than he had anticipated and fined this boy 5/- (25p). Then followed 5 youths each 19 years of age whom he fined 10/- each for disorderly conduct, but did not count the charge for damage to Sapling Service Trees, as they pleaded not guilty, but I considered the damage to be the more serious charge.

The remainder of the intruders were fined 2/- each, and I sincerely hope the Committee will give every support to the Chief Constable and myself in this matter, as these offenders must be stopped or the Park will be disfigured beyond redemption. Of course, if the Committee are going to let warning do, then I am afraid the beauty spots are soon going to be like a good deal of the remainder, a rough Recreation Ground. A great number of the Ratepayers do appreciate and respect their Park and come to admire its beauties and enjoy the fresh air, and are grievously disappointed to see the wanton destruction so plainly visible and are naturally very indignant; the Committee can rest assured they will have their warm support in any efforts to stop the destruction and waste.

One can feel nothing but sympathy for the Curator in what appears to have been an on-going battle with visitors who clearly understood what was expected of them in the Park but, equally clearly, felt that they knew better. He would, therefore, be greatly relieved by the reaction of Committee Members, who looked for further support from the Chief Constable in prosecuting offenders.

Restoration Objectives

The maintenance and improvement of the Park's infrastructure has been an on-going process from the outset and it is a crucial theme within the current Restoration Project. As far as the major east-west walkway is concerned, gaps in the trees are to be filled in in order to complete the line, while shrubs will be planted to screen off sports facilities, the pavilion and the play area. This is, in fact, part of an overall policy with regard to shrub planting and tree management, the sum of £26,500 having been allocated for the latter element alone. The Master Plan costing for the improvement of the east-west walkway scheme itself was £171,700, while that for boundary planting was £42,700.

A general Restoration Plan survey of the full network of paths within the Park led to the recommendation of the reconstruction of the following, at an estimated cost of £140,900:

- The path edges along the main axial walks and around the Fountain
- The paths along the west side and across the southern end of the Lower Lake
- The path which will form the emergency vehicular access route between the new Visitor Centre and the new vehicular entrance on the southern boundary of the Park
- The inner circuit walk where it crosses the south-western sector of the Park

Within its general infrastructure, the location and quality of all path furniture is to be reviewed, with a view to its better fitting into the overall design and layout of the Park itself. Existing seats are to be refurbished and twenty additional seats of the same design will be provided. Where visitors sit to relax, they will eat, read newspapers, smoke, and so on, and it has been decided to provide forty new litter bins. As a means of improving visitor information and circulation within the Park, six entrance signboards are to be installed, together with three strategically-positioned finger-post signs. The Master Plan costing for this overall scheme was £78,800.

As we have seen, the most crucial, literally underlying, problem relating to the preparation of the Park site at the outset was the installation of a drainage system, the maintenance of which has been a matter of on-going concern up to the present day. The sum of £288,500 has been built into the Master Plan costings in order to cater for a specialist programme of works in this respect.

Our Walk Begins

As we now embark upon our actual tour of the Park, we will consider the lay-out of the site in the four natural sectors into which it is divided by the axial walkways. The north-west division is Sector 1, the north-east is Sector 2, the south-east is Sector 3 and the south-west is Sector 4. In each case, I will note the original features and indicate the physical changes which have subsequently taken place.

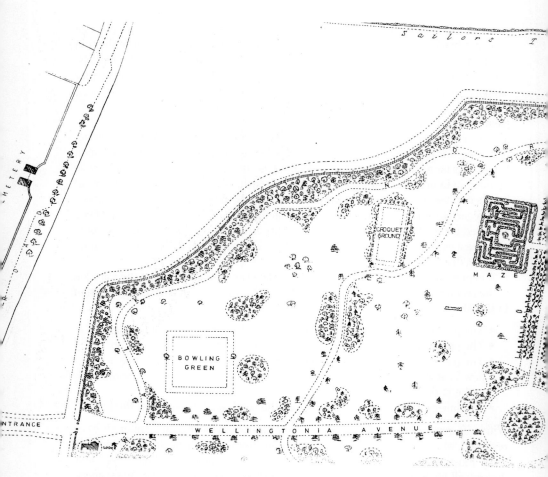

Sector 1 in 1868, showing the Bowling Green, the Croquet Ground and the Maze. Notice the entrance to the Middlesbrough Cemetery on Linthorpe Road and the blank area opposite, which was earmarked for its extension. Teesside Archives Department

SECTOR 1

The Albert Park Memorial Garden

At a time when we are celebrating the progressing of the Albert Park Restoration Project, it is very fitting that we should be welcomed at the outset of our visit by the Albert Park Memorial Garden, immediately to our left. Designed in keeping with the criteria of the Heritage Lottery Fund, it was officially opened on 2 December 2001 by Councillor Pat Walker, Mayor of Middlesbrough. The Garden was established as a co-operative venture between Middlesbrough Council and the Landing Ship Tanks and Landing Craft Association, supported by the British Legion.

During the Second World War, it was decided that the production of landing craft should be moved away from regular shipbuilders and the river Tees became an important centre for their production. From 1942, a total of 476 such vessels, and

The Albert Park Memorial Garden. Matthew Smartt

Park Road South

Cenotaph

Main Entrance Gates

Memorial Wall

New Trees

New Bedding Area

West Lodge

Clock

Existing Hedging

New Shrub Planting

Flowering Cherry

Existing Trees (to be retained)

Boundary of Memorial Garden

Royal Navy & Royal Marines Plaque

Bedding Areas

Lawn

New Low Shrub & Ground Cover Planting

Sponsor's Plaque

 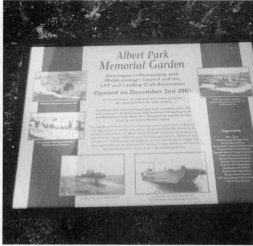

The Memorial Garden dedication stone and information board. Photos George Ward

related craft, was launched on the Tees at Middlesbrough and Stockton, in yards which were normally involved in the production of bridges and other steel structures.

It is both the efforts of the production workers and the Royal Navy personnel and Royal Marines who lost their lives while manning landing craft who are remembered and honoured in the Memorial Garden. One of its most striking features is the nineteenth century cannon, a relic of the Crimean War, the story of which will be

The Memorial Garden, with the author at the Crimean Cannon, which formerly stood at the Cannon Lake. Photo George Ward

The site of the Memorial Garden was formerly used for artistic carpet bedding displays, this one depicting the Middlesbrough coat of arms and the name of the Mayor in 1960, Alderman Walter Flynn. Photo Mr A Stephenson

The Parks Department also prepared similar displays on the Linthorpe Road frontage of Ayresome Gardens, which were laid out on the site of the old Middlesbrough cemetery. In 1987, they commemorated the centenary of the Teesside Apollo Male Voice Choir. Photo Ken Barlow

considered later, in the context of the Cannon Lake, to which it gave its name.

The Memorial Garden itself maintains a fine tradition of floral displays on this site, which was formerly used in a particularly artistic way with displays of carpet bedding. These depicted the Middlesbrough coat of arms and the name of the current Mayor of the Borough, as well as commemorating events and anniversaries of local or wider interest.

Bowling Greens

The newspaper commentator of 14 August 1868 noted as follows:

> *The bowling green, 129 feet square, is immediately reached - which will no doubt soon afford substantial enjoyment to the admirers of that ancient and not-to-be-despised game. Owing to the remarkably dry season, the strong clayey land, and the unusually hot weather we had experienced, the ground had not yet been completed in the manner intended.*

It is interesting to see at an early date that members of the public were not prepared to restrict their activities to the specifically designated areas. On 2 July 1879, it was reported to the Committee that the Bowling Green was in a poor condition and the following order was issued:

> *Ordered that the Croquet Parties be asked to remove from Bowling Green to the ground set aside for playing Croquet, and that the Bowling Green be put in a reasonable state of repair.*

That, however, was not the end of the matter and croquet players responded in writing to this decision. As a result of this groundswell of opinion, they were allowed access to the Bowling Green on Tuesdays, Thursdays and Saturdays.

The original Bowling Green was solely for the use of Bowling Club members and in 1913 it was decided that provision should also be made for a public Green in the area between the main walk and the Maze, a site also to be set aside for a pavilion. The laying of the turf, which was imported from Carlisle, was reported as completed at the Committee meeting of 17 February 1914 and the Green was officially opened on 1 July 1914 by Mrs Harry Bolckow, the wife of H W F Bolckow, nephew of the donor of the Park. On 17 June 1936, the Committee confirmed arrangements for the extension of the pavilion at the Bowling Green and for the provision of a new six-Rink Green, the latter being officially opened on 10 May 1937.

On 18 November 1938, the Borough Engineer presented a scheme for the provision of a further six-Rink Green between the main walk and the previous Green and tenders were considered on 17 February 1939. However, the Minutes do not seem to follow this through and it probably did not materialise due to the onset of the Second World War in the September of that year.

During this period, the maintenance of the greens was a very slow and tedious manual process, a fact which is recalled by Ken Sherwood. He and a colleague would use a hand fork for spiking the turf, going down to a depth of about four inches and taking up to four weeks to cover all of the greens. Their supervisor would check the depth of a hole with his pencil and Ken was in trouble if it was only three inches. On one occasion, he explained that his left instep was very sore, actually causing him to

The bowling greens maintain public interest in one of the original sporting facilities of the Park. Photo George Ward

limp for a couple of weeks or so, and Mr Gott retorted that if he did not get his fork stuck in properly something else would be sore as well... .

On 22 October 1948, the Superintendent presented proposals for the provision of a new six-Rink Green, asserting that the existing three Greens could not cope with public demand. The new Green was approved, as an addition to the existing site, and formally opened on 20 July 1950 by the Committee Chairman, Alderman Bolton.

Shelters and Pavilions

When visitors first came to the Park, they were very much at risk from the elements, in that there was no provision of shelter accommodation. This fact was highlighted in the *Middlesbrough Weekly Exchange* of 10 August 1871:

> *Amongst requirements still needed we may name a large enclosure, or series of smaller ones, where the public may safely bide over a shower of rain when it comes on, and not run the risk of a catastrophe to the toilet at present not infrequently chronicled.*

Shelters were first considered as a Park requisite in 1872, an early example being seen here at the Lower Lake. Middlesbrough Reference Library

The question of a shelter for the Park was first mentioned in Committee Minutes on 5 September 1872, when its consideration was deferred. On 9 October 1873, it was ordered that Mr Bolckow should be approached on the matter, as a result of public demand for facilities, and his reply was read to the Committee on 4 June 1874. He was clearly annoyed that his name was being bandied about within the Town Council and said that it had never been his intention to be involved in the provision of Shelter Houses. However, it became clear on 8 April 1875 that he was 'ready to go on with erections'. On 3 May 1876, a design was accepted for a shelter near the fountain. By 5 December 1877, the Committee appears to have had the bit between its teeth and resolved to advertise for designs and tenders for six rustic wooden shelters. Each was to have an area of thirty square yards and to accommodate from twenty to thirty persons.

The Minutes of 24 March 1885 refer to a shelter house near the cannon and one near the south-east corner of the Park, then on 23 February 1897 it was ordered that another one should be erected near the boating lake. On 15 March 1939, it was decided that the tea rooms should be converted into a shelter for old people, then on 22 September 1950, approval was given for the replacement of the boating lake shelter with a new one close to that site. This particular scheme seems to have been beset with problems and it was on 18 February 1955 that the completion of a shelter near the landing stage was reported to Committee.

When the new bowling green was opened in 1914, it was provided with a pavilion, which had been erected at a cost of £200. In October 1952, it was decided that this

New bowling greens were opened in 1914, together with a purpose-built sports pavilion.
Middlesbrough Leisure Services

The original pavilion was replaced by the present building in early 1994, after being damaged by fire. Photo George Ward

pavilion should be temporarily converted for use as separate shelter accommodation for men and women and this proved to be such a popular move that it was repeated for several years during the winter period. The needs of the disabled were considered in March 1957 and on 20 December of the same year it was decided that suitable accommodation should be added to the pavilion. It was replaced by the present building in early 1994 after being seriously damaged by fire.

The Croquet Ground

The following paragraph appeared in the newspaper description of the Park in 1868:

> *The croquet ground is next reached. It is planted round with trees and shrubs to form a retired shelter; it is very tastefully laid out, and will only possibly be found too small for the number to join in this popular game. Like the bowling green it is full of large fissures in the clay, for want of moisture.*

As we have seen, the writer's prediction relating to the inadequacy of the site was to prove to be correct and it appears that the formal arrangements whereby the croquet players were given joint access to the Bowling Green must have worked well. By 1881, Middlesbrough Rovers Football Club must have felt that the Croquet Ground was under-used. With effect from 17 September, they were given permission to play there, 'subject to the supervision of the Curator'.

On 22 May 1894, it was proposed by the Park Committee that the Croquet Ground should be given over for the use of tennis players, but the suggestion was turned down by the Town Council and the Croquet Ground was subsequently no longer referred to in the Committee Minutes.

The Maze

> *Adjoining this walk* (the northern section of the Italian Walk) *upon the west side is a maze, laid out upon the famous plan of that at Hampton Court. When the hedges get up to 5 or 6 feet in height, it will be a maze indeed.' (*Middlesbrough and Stockton Gazette *14 August 1868)*

One of the more unusual features of the Park, the maze was also to prove to be one of the least successful. Three years after the official opening of the Park, it was clear that it was not 'a maze indeed', the *Middlesbrough Weekly Exchange* of 10 August 1871 reporting that *'The labyrinth appears to be quite a failure on the north side and will have to be re-planted'*. In its issue of 18 May 1881, the same newspaper reported that *'it is satisfactory to find that the labyrinth will in a few years be ready for use'*, while by 6 September 1883 it was still a matter of looking to the future. In his fascinating article in that particular issue, 'A Rambler' stated that

> the *'maze'* is growing well, the hedges being now of a good height, and it is probable that next spring it may be ready for the admission of visitors, who may choose to lose themselves in its perplexing intricacies.

As it happened, the writer was ten years out in his aspirations, for it was not until 11 August 1894 that the maze was officially opened by Alderman Scupham, Chairman of the Park Committee. It was appropriate that the ceremony took place on the anniversary of the official opening of the Park itself, but most unfortunate that it was twenty-six years after that event. During the course of his speech, Alderman Scupham expressed the following sentiments, as reported in the *North Eastern Daily Gazette* of 11 August:

> He hoped the public would appreciate the maze, and remember that it was public property, and that they would each treat it as if it belonged to themselves, and see that no one destroyed any part of it.

On 28 August, within a fortnight of the official opening, the Curator reported to the Committee that there had been no damage to the hedges, but that the footpaths were in a very poor condition because of the wet weather. Within a year however, he was reporting on actual damage to the hedges as well as wear and tear to the paths.

On 19 December 1911, the Curator was instructed to produce a report on the maze and this was presented to Committee on 16 January 1912:

> In accordance with your instructions I have to report that the Maze covers an area of 2,304 square yards. It has been open to the Public for about 15 years, from July to November, it has always been the rule not to open it before July, so as to give the Birds a chance of nesting, as they are pretty safe here from Boys robbing them. The walks have got worn pretty badly in places as they are nothing but clay and require making. There is a great amount of damage done every year to the Hedges by children, when they get into the centre they will not walk back the proper way, but break through the outer Hedges. There has been no record kept of the number of people who visit the Maze.

The writing was clearly on the wall (or the hedge) for the maze and in a subsequent report on 18 November 1913 the Curator reaffirmed the problem of wilful damage by children, with an additional statement:

> It also takes a man about 12 weeks each year to clip and repair the same; also during the time it is open it takes a good deal of a man's time watching it.

On 16 January 1914, the Committee decided that the maze should be closed to the public for the time being and there is no record of it ever being re-opened before, on 9 July 1919, it was ordered to be abolished. It can be imagined that tastes in fashion and demands on space may well have led to the disappearance of the maze, but it is a sad indictment on a certain element within the general body of visitors that its demise was brought about through misuse. We may feel that vandalism in public places is a modern phenomenon, but that is clearly not the case.

The maze was still featured on the Ordnance Survey map of 1915, but the site itself now forms part of the bowling greens. The Restoration Master Plan makes no recommendation for its reinstatement, but it can be noted in passing that there is some interest in creating an embankment formation on the same principle.

Tennis and Tennis Courts

The principal sporting activity in Sector 1 is now tennis, the Park origins of which are not clear. There is a passing reference to lawn tennis in the article by 'A Rambler' in the *Middlesbrough Daily Exchange* of 6 September 1883, but it does not feature in the Park Committee Minutes until 27 September 1892, when the condition of the courts was a matter of concern. Two years later, as noted above, there was an unsuccessful bid by the Park Committee to allow tennis to be played on the Croquet Ground.

On 21 February 1912, it was reported that eight courts were then available to the public and it was decided not to go ahead with the proposed provision of two more. On 22 September 1913, the Curator referred to a Tennis Ground known as the *Bowling Green* and recommended its extension so that this ground would provide six double courts. The year 1925 saw the introduction of plans for the provision of an unspecified number of hard courts, which were officially opened on 19 September.

In the post-War years, attention turned to the provision of all-weather courts, four

Tennis in the Park is first mentioned in 1883 and the present courts now represent the major sporting activity in Sector 1. Photo George Ward

of which were reported as having been completed by 24 March 1950. They were formally opened by the Chairman, Alderman Bolton, on 20 July of the same year. A further unspecified number of courts was in use by 21 October 1955.

The Putting Green

In early 1925, plans were being considered for establishing a putting green in the midst of the bowling greens and tennis courts. On 17 February, the Curator suggested to the Park Committee that consideration should be given to allocating funds for fitting out the new green, estimating that the cost of equipment would be approximately £120.

At the Park Committee Meeting of 21 April, the Curator apologised for the fact that the green would not be ready for use as soon as he had anticipated, now expecting that it would be ready by June. In the meantime, he had made enquiries about charges on eighteen-hole greens and felt that the common 2d per person per round was a very reasonable sum. The Committee ordered that this was to be the charge in Albert Park.

On 15 September, the Curator reported that work on the putting green had been completed and that it was due to be officially opened on the 19th of that month.

The Picnic Area

One of the attractions, albeit seasonal, of being in the Park is that of being able to eat al fresco, and with that in mind, the provision of the picnic area has been a boon for visitors of all ages.

In the Stage One Restoration Plan, consideration was given to the idea of moving the picnic facilities to another part of the Park, but it was subsequently decided to maintain the status quo. In order to improve its setting, however, the railings which separate the existing picnic area from the bowling greens are to be extended and it

Visitors can spend a pleasantly relaxing time in the picnic area, as a break from their tour of the Park. Photo George Ward

will benefit from the re-planting of the West Walk and the Italian Garden. The Master Plan costing for this scheme was £7,800.

The Prehistoric Tree Trunk and Boulder

Another natural advantage of a public park is that it provides a setting for an open-air museum and Albert Park proved to be of interest in this respect at an early period. A site on the southern fringe of Sector 1, opposite the West Lodge, was set aside for the display of two ancient relics which had both been removed from the river Tees.

The Park Committee Minutes of 26 March 1872 refer to the need to obtain an inscribed plate for the trunk of a prehistoric oak which had recently been dredged from the river and presented to them for display in the Park, where it was placed on its side. It proved to be an object of more than historical interest to youngsters of several generations, who used its steep side as a slide. Many a trouser seat, including my own, gave the ancient timber a good polishing. Given my present feeling for 'touching the past', it is amusing to think of starting the habit at such an early age and with such an unusual part of my anatomy!

In January 1950, the recommendations of the Parks Superintendent were accepted with regard to measures for the improvement of the appearance of the area inside the main gates and it was decided that the tree trunk should be removed. This happened in November 1951 , when it was moved to the children's playground at the east end of the Park. Since that time, it has disappeared. At the time of its removal, the following worn inscription was noted on the plate fixed to it in 1872:

> *This tree is part of the oak forest*   *Tees*
> *Conservancy Commissioners*   *South side of*
> *the River Tees opposite to the Eston Iron Works in*
> *the years 1870-71. It weighed eleven tons when it*
> *was placed here in the presence of*
> *H W F Bolckow, Esq, MP*

It is worthy of note that in 1925 Henry Bolckow's statue was to be placed near the

The prehistoric tree trunk which was dredged from the river Tees and installed in the Park in 1872, close to the present site of the Crimean Cannon. Nearby was the ancient boulder, another relic from the Tees.   Paul Stephenson Collection

tree trunk, remaining there for some sixty years. The whole question of the provision of a permanent memorial in the Park in honour of Henry Bolckow is considered in Chapter Six.

Associated with the ancient tree trunk was a large boulder from the Tees at Newport. It bore a plate with the following inscription:

> *This stone was dredged from the*
> *River Tees at Newport A. D. 1869*
> *and is believed to be one of the*
> *Stepping Stones of the Ancient*
> *Ford at Newport*

This, in itself, was another object of great interest to the younger generation and it was also well-polished by countless juvenile bottoms. After its removal in 1951, it was transferred to the collections of the Dorman Memorial Museum for safekeeping. Since the recent moving of the Crimean cannon, it now stands alone to the west of the main entrance.

The Sun Dial

Just a few years after the installation of the tree trunk and boulder in the Park, a site to their east was set aside for the erection of an elegant sun dial. The first reference to it in the Park Committee Minutes appears on 4 January 1879:

> *A letter having been received from Mr. Bolckow's steward asking the Committee to fix a position for the new Sun Dial, it was ordered that it be fixed where the Notice Board now is, on the left side of the walk inside the main entrance.*

The sun dial was actually designed and manufactured by John Smith of South Stockton (modern Thornaby), who was self-taught in the art. Once erected, it proved to be a source of great interest to visitors, as is shown by the following paragraph in the *Middlesbrough Daily Exchange* of 18 May 1881:

> *There have been but few additions of any moment made to the attractions of the park since last season. The sun dial near the principal entrance into Albert Park, the gift of the late Mr Bolckow, is the last striking addition that the Park Committee have had to record. It is not only an interesting but a useful object, and so great a curiosity is it regarded to be that the numbers of people who visit the park, and whose first object is to read the dial and its inscriptions, have worn away the grass at the base of the dial, a fact which leads one to make the suggestion that a railing round the base would be a great improvement, and would tend to preserve the stone structure from any risk of injury. The ingenious designer of the dial which amongst other things tells the time as it is simultaneously in London, New York and Melbourne, is Mr John Smith, of Stockton-upon-Tees. Many of the inscriptions are very quaint, and well calculated to arrest the attention. The equation table would be none the worse if it were painted, so that the figures were made more distinct.*

On 29 November 1881, it was reported to Committee by the Borough Surveyor that the iron railing round the sun dial was then in position. Two years later, on 6

The sun dial was erected in 1879, as a gift from Henry Bolckow. The box hedge was later replaced by railings. Middlesbrough Reference Library

September 1883, the *Middlesbrough Daily Exchange* article by 'A Rambler' contained the following remarks:

> *Passing through the ornamental gates at the principal entrance, in Linthorpe-road, my attention was attracted by the curious sun-dial constructed by Mr John Smith, of Stockton, which was erected at the expense of the late Mr Bolckow, M. The structure bears the date 1879, but I think its erection did not take place till 1880. Anyway, it must be an object of interest to visitors, not only of its correct notation of solar time, but for the quaint mottoes and proverbs which cover its face.*

In the Department of the Environment *List of Buildings of Special Architectural or Historical Interest* (1988), the sun dial has a Grade II listing, and it is described thus:

> *Sundial dated 1876 and 1879, by John Smith (Stockton), for H W F Bolckow (ironmaster). Sandstone ashlar; bronze gnomon. Gothic style. Sundial inscribed*

The sun dial was designed to show the time in London, New York and Melbourne and is still of great interest to the public. Dorman Museum

on painted tablet, dated 1876, under segmental-pointed recess, in pilaster-and-gable surround. Roundel in gable dated 1879. Deep plinth has gabled angle buttresses and slate tablet inscribed: 'Equation of Time for Every 5th Day of the Month, followed by table. Sundial has concentric dials, giving time in New York, Melbourne and the Park. Greek mottoes in spandrels. Square border inscribed: 'TIME BY MOMENTS STEALS AWAY FIRST THE HOUR THEN THE DAY'. Diagram of solar system above dials, with 12 signs of zodiac in oval border. Below sundial, verse now partly eroded. Blank panel in similar surround on reverse side. Dilapidated at time of resurvey.

The final remark is both blunt and telling. In stating the obvious, it highlights the reason for the inclusion of the sun dial in the group of historic structures ear-marked for attention in the Restoration Project. In their May 2000 survey, Hirst Conservation's description of the actual structure brings us echoes of that above, but more pertinent here are the comments relating to its actual condition:

- The sandstone is heavily polluted with carbon deposits as a result of heavy local industrial and airborne hydrocarbons. Due to the architectural design, constant run-off of rain may be exacerbating the decay. Erosion and salt migration has badly damaged the face of the sundial.
- The sundial was originally fenced around. Later the fence was removed and a hedge planted. The hedge has since been removed and the sundial does not have any protection.
- The sun dial stands directly on the ground, which may be allowing harmful salts such as nitrates to migrate through the stone. This will be exacerbated from the urine from dogs, given the location and exposed position.

Time itself has not been kind to the sun dial, which is now scheduled for restoration. Photo George Ward

- Previous attempts to point the structure have been carried out in a dark, hard cementitious mortar and in many places open joints exist. Some joints are failing altogether.
- Algae and lichen growth are evident on the surface and would need to be removed during the cleaning process.
- There is some impact damage to the sun dial. Most of these are chips from the structure.

The sun dial has clearly suffered from atmospheric pollution after being exposed to the elements for over 120 years and it would appear that previous attempts at conservation may have done as much harm as good. As we saw earlier, this structure proved to be of great interest to many of those interviewed during the on-site survey, and its restoration is bound be a very popular development.

The South African War Memorial

Further east from the sun dial is situated the obelisk of the South African War Memorial, which, like the Dorman Memorial Museum, honours local men who died during the Boer War of 1899–1902.

At their meeting of 24 November 1903, the Park Committee considered a letter from the Middlesbrough War Memorial Fund Committee, with a proposal to erect a war memorial in Victoria Square. On 23 February 1904, the Committee turned it down, feeling that it could be more suitably situated in the Park. By 18 May, agreement had been reached relating to its present site and the elegant obelisk was

unveiled on 7 June 1905 by Lieut-General Sir Henry Leslie Randle.

In the Department of the Environment *List of Buildings of Special Architectural or Historical Interest* (1988), the South African Memorial is given a Grade II listing and is described thus:

South African War Memorial, 1904, by F W Doyle Jones (Hartlepool). Red Peterhead granite, York stone steps, and bronze tablets. Obelisk, with linked volutes and bay-leaf swags at base, on tapered pedestal with heavily-moulded cornice. Moulded stepped base with bay-leaf and cyma-recta moulding on top step. 3 plain lower steps. Sculptured tablets, on north and south faces of die, depict fame (south) and patriotism. Names of fallen on raised-lettered tablet on west face. Included for historic interest.

The South African War Memorial, which was unveiled on 7 June 1905.
Photo George Ward

There was no adverse reaction to the condition of the War Memorial in 1988 and it was regarded by Hirst Conservation as being generally good. The following points indicate the areas where conservation will be necessary:

- The polished red granite is in good condition with the exception of occasional chips, which require no remedial action.
- The granite is discoloured by pollutants, particularly noticeable to upstands or projecting features.
- The monument is in close proximity to trees, which may cause deposits and deterioration.
- Pink paint has been daubed over part of the bay leaf garland and to a corner of the steps. Algal presence is more noticeable at the base of the obelisk.
- The three steps leading up to the memorial have moved and joints opened, creating a large gap.

As we saw earlier, the new Memorial Garden maintains the tradition of high quality horticulture in Sector 1, another fine example of which was undertaken in the area between the South African War Memorial and the fountain in the year 1955.

The Former Garden of Fragrance
On 10 June of that year, a letter was presented to the Parks Committee from the Rotary Club of Middlesbrough, which was then considering plans to celebrate the Golden Jubilee of the International Rotary Movement. Members of the Club offered to pay for the creation of a Rest Garden for the Blind, 'with aromatic plants and with

The former Garden of Fragrance, which was situated between the South African War Memorial and the fountain. Paul Stephenson Collection

seating accommodation, subject to satisfactory arrangements regarding the site and form.' The offer was gratefully accepted and it was ordered that the matter should be taken forward with the Rotary Club.

In September 1955, the Chairman of the Rotary Club, Sir Edward Anderson, JP, stated that his members hoped to raise £350 for the project, but it was costed out at £461, with additional expenditure for labels in braille. At this same time, it was decided that it would be more appropriate if the garden were to be known as 'A Garden of Fragrance', so that nobody would feel that they were not entitled to use the facilities. Given that the Rotary Club was not prepared to simply make a contribution towards a much greater sum, an amended estimate of £376 was produced in October for a revised scheme and this was accepted, on the understanding that a suitable plaque would be installed in the Garden as an acknowledgement of the Rotary Club's sponsorship of the scheme.

The Fountain
The description of the Park in the *Middlesbrough and Stockton Gazette* of 14 August 1868 contains the following reference to the mound which occupied the central site at the junction of the four principal walkways:

Proceeding down this (the Wellingtonia) *walk, we reach the centre mound, 96*

The fountain was presented by Joseph Pease of Darlington in 1869 and is seen here not long after its installation. The villas in the background later became the Middlesbrough Maternity Home on Park Road North. Teesside Archives Department

feet across, encircled by an asphalted promenade 46 feet wide and 1,000 feet long, taking the centre of the path. The mound is planted with Rhododendrons, and kindred varieties of ornamental foliage. The outer edge of the foliage is already well planted by beds of trees and shrubs in a very forward state of growth.

It has already been noted that this mound was originally ear-marked for the erection of statuary, but it was never, in fact, used for that purpose. Instead, it presented itself as an ideal situation for an ornamental fountain, the gift of Joseph Pease of Darlington. During her researches, Linda Polley found it impossible to trace the actual origins of the fountain, but she has made the interesting suggestion that it may have been purchased at an exhibition, in the same way that Henry Bolckow had acquired the main entrance gates.

On 6 May 1869, it was reported to the Park Committee that work had begun on removing the earth of the mound in order to make way for the foundations of the fountain and work on its actual construction was carried out during the Summer. The *Middlesbrough Weekly News and Cleveland Advertiser* of 9 July reported that:

The granite rim of Mr Pease's fountain in the centre of the park is just finished and apparently the fountain may be in full play in the course of a fortnight or so, and will be a handsome ornament.

On 22 October of the same year, the Park Committee decided that the following simple inscription should be placed on the fountain itself:

Presented by Joseph Pease 1869

Unfortunately, however, the donor did not live to see the fixing of the plate, as he died in 1872, and it was to be another nine years before the matter was mentioned again at Committee. On 30 August 1881, it was ordered that the brass plate should be put in place, then on 27 September it was reported that this would be done in time for the celebration of Middlesbrough's Jubilee, which was to take place on 6 October. By that time, there had been a change of plan relating to the wording of the actual inscription, which was as follows:

This Fountain was presented to the adornment of the Albert Park by Joseph Pease Esq. October 1869.

It appears that the actual operation of the fountain was an expensive business and it is clear that maintenance was a recurring problem from quite an early period. By

Known as Parkside, the former Maternity Home building was later acquired by the University of Teeside and is pictured in January 2002. Photo George Ward

November 1910, the Park Committee had decided to lay new water pipes to the fountain, but in 1927 the situation was even more serious. The Curator presented the following report at the meeting of 18th January:

CENTRAL FOUNTAIN

As ordered at your last Meeting I submit a Report with respect to the repairs necessary to put the above Fountain into proper working order. In my opinion it is the internal pipes that are at fault, being corroded to such an extent that very little water can pass through. These pipes will need dismantling and cleaning, or possibly replacing with new piping.

The trouble at this Fountain began many years ago; it was then thought that the old main was at fault, as cracked portions taken out for replacement were found to be in a very corroded state indeed. You decided to lay a new main in the hope this would rectify the bad force at the Fountain, but this had not the effect anticipated, for the force was no better, and this convinces me that the internal pipes need attention. The basin is also badly cracked and needs repairing, for when last filled, it went down nearly six inches in one night. I venture to suggest the basin be filled up with a foot or more of concrete, as it is certainly too deep at present and has proved to be a positive danger, for on one or two occasions children have fallen in and nearly drowned before they could be rescued. Apart from this, it would take less water and the Fountain could then be played more regularly, which would be very much appreciated by Park visitors. I suggest the Borough Engineer be asked to examine and get out an approximate cost of necessary repairs, and recommend the amount be included in the new Estimates, so that this Fountain may be put into thorough working order.

The Curator also reported that the drain from the fountain into the North Lake was useless, being completely blocked, and that it was necessary to empty the basin on to the public footpath. The Committee ordered that his recommendations relating to a report from the Borough Engineer should be implemented, but there does not appear to have been any follow-up to this.

Two decades later, the Minutes of the Parks Committee highlight the fact that the maintenance and repair of the fountain was an on-going problem, to the extent that adventurous children were very much at risk. The following report, which was presented by the Superintendent on 22 October 1948, is particularly worthy of note:

RENOVATION OF FOUNTAIN – ALBERT PARK. – As instructed by the Committee, I am pleased to submit the following observations and recommendations for the improvement of the Fountain and the immediate vicinity, which constitutes the central ornamental feature of the Albert Park.

For a considerable time, the fountain has been in an unserviceable condition, the metal being corroded beyond repair, and the surrounding basin has constituted a pool of stagnant water which is unhealthy in the extreme. The outlet has been made up as a result of which it has been impossible to prevent children from paddling in the polluted water and risking damage to their feet by broken glass and stones, and incidentally doing serious damage to clothing.

With the co-operation of the Borough Engineer, sections of the fountain which

The elegant upper column and embellishments of the fountain were later removed, but will be replicated as part of the Park Restoration Project. Photo George Ward

were beyond repair have been removed, and it is hoped to have what now remains re-designed in the near future. The basin has also been emptied and cleaned, and the old and unsuitable rock foundation has also been removed.

I propose that, upon the reconstruction of the fountain, the existing curb be removed and replaced by a suitable wall not more than 18 inches in height, above which the play of the fountain could be seen from the main public footpath some 25 ft. away. I would also suggest the removal of the inner footpath in order to keep the children from playing in the fountain water, and also to make possible the construction of a new central feature consisting of flower beds and turf. The inner footpath is serving no useful purpose, and the proposed feature could be constructed and maintained by the existing staff at a negligible cost.

Approval was given for the Superintendent's recommendations to be put into effect and the work was reported completed at the Committee meeting of 10 June 1949. After all that hard work, and subsequent maintenance, the fountain has continued to have its problems up to the present time. The visitor survey carried out in the Summer of 1997 revealed considerable public support for the restoration of the fountain, which the Consultants' Submission Document of June 2000 describes as an 'exuberant historic feature that has lost a substantial part of its fabric.' It is, most certainly, a significant Park feature which is worthy of full restoration. The Master

Plan costing for this scheme was £63,100 and the Submission Document makes the following observations:

> There are excellent photographic records of the fountain, of which only the lower bowl now survives. The photographs show the missing features to be highly ornamental and richly detailed with herons, swans and lily leaves. Alternative, similar style, more cost effective catalogue fountains have been researched but with no success, so, on the basis of the photographic evidence along with two of the herons (which survive), the approach will be to create a replica of the original fountain, reproducing the original detailing as faithfully as possible.

The two extant herons were actually handed over to the Friends of Albert Park as an anonymous gift, which means that there is no way of knowing where they have been kept since their removal from the fountain. Attempts to trace the other pair have so far met with no success.

Two of the original four cast iron herons from the fountain have been returned anonymously to the Friends of Albert Park. They are to be replicated so that this significant feature can be completely restored. Photo George Ward

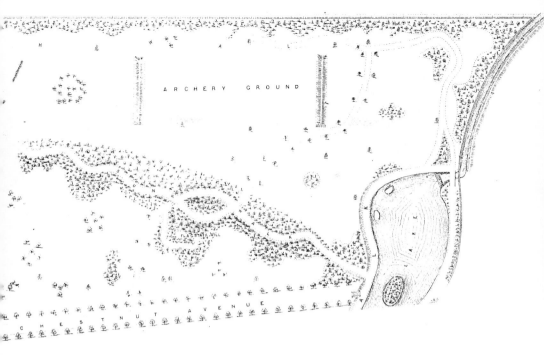

The main features of the Sector 2 area of the 1868 plan were the Archery Ground and the landscaped area of the Sunk Walk and the Bell Hill. Teesside Archives Department

SECTOR 2

The Italian Garden

The north-south axis of the Park, bisecting the two main walks at the fountain, has been variously described as a floral walk, an Italian Walk or an Italian Garden, and proved to be a showcase for the horticultural skills of the Curator and his staff from the outset. It was of considerable interest to Victorian journalistic commentators, particularly 'A Rambler', writing in the *Middlesbrough Daily Exchange* of 6 September 1883:

> *Coming now to the floral walk, or Italian garden, which stretches north and south through the park, I notice that it is just now in the height of perfection. At the south end there are two large beds of sub-tropical plants, exactly alike – in fact, I may remark that the beds on each side of the walk throughout are as nearly as possible counterpart of each other. In the centre of each bed is a magnificent castor oil plant, surrounded by the purple foliage of the* perella nancunencis, *or dark heath plant. This again is bordered by a layer of hamiog geraniums, outside of which are tregetas, and the azure lobelia and the delicate-hued cirastia form the outer circle. Along the borders of the path there are two descriptions of beds. Those in the centre are diamond-shaped, while oblong beds flank them on each side. In the centre beds may chiefly be noticed the peculiar foliage of the Indian shot, as well as the trentum rose geranium, the pink nose (sic), the yellow geranium, the blue hygeratum, the cineraria, and the maritinum white. In every fifth bed is a specimen of the clematis Jackmani, which is now in great beauty – the plants being almost hidden in purple bloom. It is often considered by gardeners that this plant will not succeed so far*

The Italian Walk divides the Park from north to south, the southern section being seen here after the installation of the first band stand in 1871. The top-hatted gent is believed to be Edward Cleaton, the first Curator, with his crinolined wife centre and one of their sons manning the lawnmower on the floral border to her left. Teesside Archives Department and Author's Collection

north, but here is has withstood the rigours of winter for six years past, and is in better condition than ever. In one bed I noticed a layer of the golden-leaved nasturtium, which is very much admired by visitors, and is very rare in the district. Throughout the whole parterre the blending of colour is very good indeed, no tint being unduly prominent; but a more lavish use of white and yellow in the centre beds will probably improve their appearance. The plants are so arranged as to avoid a formal appearance, and to give the best effect to the pyramidal plants.

The effects of time and tender loving care are evident in the engraving of about 1900. Teesside Archives Department and Author's Collection

At the time of the official opening of the Park, a much briefer reference is, nevertheless, still of interest, for it gives us the original dimensions of that section of the Italian walk which divides Sectors 1 and 2:

> *The north portion of the walk is 540 feet long, and 14 feet wide, and for the entire length is laid out upon each side, in a festooned chain border, from an original design by Mr Cleeton.*

It has been said that a wooden floor in the West Lodge, Edward Cleaton's residence, had been used as a drawing-board for his designs, the chalk outlines of which were later discovered underneath the carpet.

Described in the Restoration Submission Document as a 'dramatic and historic ornamental axis', the Italian Garden is also regarded as 'a crucial element of the original design'. In view of its status, and based upon the evidence of archival photographs and plans, the original bedding design is to be re-created, as a means of introducing a 'greater diversity and richness of experience to the Park'.

The estimated cost of this scheme was £199,400.

The Sunk Walk and The Bell Hill

The lowest point of the entire Park site is at its eastern extremity, where the Lower Lake was excavated, an exercise which must have produced many tons of spoil. The highest point of the site is the Bell Hill, which took its name from the bell which was rung there as a public warning of the imminent closure of the Park. One of the principal features of Sector 2 to the west of the lake, it was almost certainly created from its spoil, as also would be the three islands on the lake itself. Another source of earth for this hill would be from the excavation of the Sunk Walk, or Swiss Walk, which gave access to it from the west.

This landscaped area is one of the original features of the Park and the following interesting description appeared in the *Middlesbrough and Stockton Gazette* of 14 August 1868:

> *Opposite the entrance to the maze is the Swiss walk, 14 feet wide, which we will now take. It winds gracefully through some hills, planted with oak, ash, elm, poplar, &c, with a luxuriant undergrowth of shrubs. When the trees get into maturity, there will be alike a cool refuge from the sun, with sultriest beams, and a protected refuge in the winter, when 'from the north the fierce winds blow'. We next reach a circular mound planted with ornamental trees upon the top, and upon the sides with the variegated acuba japonica, producing a very fine effect. Ascending a flight of steps to the right of the walk, a winding path leads to the top of the hill – the highest point in the grounds –*

> > *'How lovely from this hill's superior height,*
> > *Spreads the wide scene before the straining sight!'*

> *Commanding views of the whole of the park, and the surrounding landscape in every direction – the ships upon the river, railway trains passing in all directions, the ironworks of the district, Stockton with its churches, the Cleveland hills, Captain Cook's monument, Roseberry Topping, the Hambledon Hills, and the distant ocean – a magnificent panorama.*

The Bell Hill is the highest landscaped point in the Park and was formerly the site of the warning bell which was rung prior to closing time. Photo George Ward

In September 1969, work began on the cleaning of the Lower Lake, an exercise which was to have a serious effect on the Sunk Walk and the Bell Hill. Ken Sherwood has described how masses of slurry were removed from the bed of the lake and transported to the Bell Hill for disposal. This produced an area of a porridge-like consistency, some ten feet deep, with a thin dry crust, and it was necessary to double-fence the site because of the obvious danger to the public.

It can be assumed that it was this project which led to the in-filling and levelling of the Sunk Walk, a situation which has led to the formulation of a future scheme as an extension of the current Restoration Programme. There is to be a community-based archaeological investigation of the alignment of the original path and its levels, which will be restored where possible. Shrubs, bulbs and longer grass will be planted and the nearby playground railings are to be re-aligned in order to improve the setting of the Sunk Walk. The Master Plan costing for this scheme was £56,000. In association with the recreation of this original Park feature, a small sculpture or paving pattern is to be introduced on the crest of the Bell Hill, as a reminder of the former location there of the warning bell.

The Mary Cooper Murder

In the year 1884, the peace and beauty of this high spot were violated in a way which was to have a long-term effect on parents' attitudes to their children being in that area of the Park. This related to the disappearance and tragic re-discovery of eight-year-old Mary Cooper, who lived with her family in Waterloo Road.

Mary had gone to the Park on 21 June of that year to play with her two younger sisters, staying with them until lunch-time. The girls then became separated and Mary was never seen alive again. Several searches were made in the Park, including the lakes, but it was two days before her body was found at the Bell Hill. Her throat had been cut and her face and clothing were covered in dried blood. She was lying on her

Mary Cooper, standing left, of Waterloo Road, Middlesbrough, who was murdered on the Bell Hill in June 1884. Mrs Waites

back, her eyes open, and there were clumps of grass in each hand, one arm being by her side and the other above her head.

The following reference to Mary's brutal death appeared in the report of Chief Constable Saggerson, which he presented to the Watch Committee on 24 June 1884:

> *Gentlemen, – I am sorry to inform you that a little girl, eight years of age, named Mary Cooper, who resided with her parents at 56 Waterloo Road, was found Murdered near the Bell Mound, in the Park, at about 4.30 p.m. yesterday.*
>
> *The girl had been missing from her home since noon on Saturday last. I beg most respectfully to recommend that the Corporation, at once, offer a Reward of £100 to any person or persons giving such information as will lead to the apprehension and conviction of the murderer or murderers.*

Little Mary was buried in Linthorpe Cemetery and, in spite of considerable Press publicity her killer was never found. The Park Committee offered the proposed reward of £100 for information leading to a conviction, and the matter was taken further at a Special Meeting of the Town Council on 8 July, On that occasion, it was ordered that:

> *the Mayor and Town Clerk be authorised to communicate with the Home Secretary, with a view to inducing the Government to offer an additional Reward for such information as will lead to the apprehension and conviction of the Murderer or Murderers of Mary Cooper.*

Having been aware of this murder for many years, I witnessed an unusual and unnerving echo of the tragic event during my time as Local History Officer for

Cleveland County Council, when I was based in Middlesbrough Reference Library. A lady came in to see me one day with what I expected to be a routine enquiry, but it was not as simple as that.

She asked me if there had ever been a murder in Albert Park and I brought out the Mary Cooper file so that she could read the contemporary newspaper reports for herself. I sat with her as she studied them and it became clear that she was distressed, to the point of almost fainting. She explained that, when a youngster herself, some friends with her in the Park had dared her to go on to the Bell Hill. As she did so, she was confronted by the figure of a little girl in a white pinafore dress, which was stained red all down the front.

Based on my own inexperience in such matters, I do not believe in ghosts, and it could possibly be argued that local legend and a vivid imagination might have had this effect. However, as my visitor assured me that she had had no prior knowledge of Mary Cooper's murder, there was no reason to doubt her sincerity. What was clear was the fact that her own distress was genuine.

The Archery Ground

On the northern flank of the Bell Hill was the Archery Ground, another original feature which attracted the attention of our commentator in 1868:

> *Returning to the Swiss walk, we continue our way to a flight of steps leading to the archery ground, 540 feet in length and about 240 feet wide, where ladies and gentlemen may make their appearance for a contest, armed with the bow, string, arrow, glove and brace, show their proficiency in standing, knocking, drawing, holding and loosing, and their qualifications as archers by hitting the gold, red, inner-white, or black. Should any one be so unfortunate as to miss an outer-white, the embankment constructed at either end of the ground will stop the arrows – and doubtless they will sometimes be brought into requisition.*

The writer of the article in the *Middlesbrough Weekly Exchange* of 10 August 1871 relating to activities in the Park makes no reference at all to the Archery Ground and there appears to be no evidence from any source to suggest that it was, in fact, ever used by budding Robin Hoods or Will Scarletts. Even though it was stated in the Park Committee Minutes of 9 March 1871 that 'This ground to be used for the purpose designed', it would appear that it was simply given over to other sporting activities.

There is one fact about the Archery Ground which should be engraved upon the hearts and minds of all supporters of Middlesbrough Football Club, which was established in February 1876. The Club's first match actually took place on the Archery Ground on 3 March of the following year and, in that respect, it is to be regarded as hallowed ground. Within a year, however, matches were attracting crowds of over 200 and the Park Committee expressed its concern over the potential detrimental effect on the Archery Ground. The Football Club was, therefore, asked to find an alternative venue and severed its brief association with the Park. A field at Breckon Hill was subsequently used for matches, then part of the Cricket Ground on Linthorpe Road was made available. The purpose-built ground at Ayresome Park was opened in 1903 and finally the present Riverside Stadium came into use in 1995.

It would appear that there had not been a complete ban on the use of the Archery

Ground for football and the following report from the Curator to the Committee is of interest, being presented on 23 December 1879:

> *Gentlemen, – I beg to inform you that the Archery Ground has been so much used by Football players that it is not in a fit state to play on. I should recommend playing to be discontinued for the present, and the ground covered over, an inch or so, with the sand &c that was taken out of the Lower Lake, about four years ago, and sown over with grass seeds in April next.*

Members accepted the Curator's advice and all footballing activities were suspended. It is clear, however, that the Archery Ground was back in use for football in 1881, when cricket was also being played there. On 26 July of the same year, the Park Committee recorded its agreement that the Middlesbrough Lacrosse Club could also have access to the Archery Ground. Permission was later given for the staging of another minority sport, when, on 27 June 1893, it was agreed that the Baseball Club could play there. It is good to see that the youth of Middlesbrough was not overlooked in terms of access to the Archery Ground, for on 16 March 1909 it was decreed that schoolboys up to fourteen years of age could play supervised cricket there.

The Miniature Golf Course

Forty years later, an area to the east of the Archery Ground was set aside for the construction of a miniature golf course. On 23 September 1949, the Parks Committee was informed that work was under way on the green for the course, utilising surplus turf from the new tennis courts. The course was officially opened by the Chairman during a Committee visit to the Park on 26 July 1950.

Miniature golf was also referred to as 'Pitch and Putt' and the charge was 6d per person for a round of eighteen holes. Players were provided with a putter and mashie, there being an additional deposit of 1/- to cover possible loss of the ball. Tickets were issued in strict rotation and it was not possible to make a reservation. The course was available to the public each day during the season, dependent upon the condition of the green.

The poor condition and ill-defined lay-out of what is now referred to as a putting green was a matter of concern for the Restoration Consultants. It is anticipated that its improvement, as a longer-term project, will increase public interest in this under-used facility.

The North Lake

Within the original concept of the Park design, there was provision for two stretches of water – the Upper and Lower Lakes – which will be considered as our tour continues. Within a year of the official opening, plans were in hand for the creation of a third lake, to be situated to the west of the Archery Ground, in the north-west corner of Sector 2.

At the Park Committee meeting held of 10 April 1869, it was ordered that 'a lake be excavated on the north side of the Park on the site where there now exists a partial excavation' and the work was reported completed at the meeting of 6 January 1870. In late 1877, it was decided to extend the lake and on 6 February 1878 it was ordered that slag removed from the former Exhibition Ground on the south side of

The North Lake, which was excavated in 1869 and filled in in 1951. Derek Enderby Collection

the Park (see Sector 3) should be used for the banking. Fish for the lake were provided by Mr Hustler of Acklam Hall and it was reported on 2 April 1879 that the alterations were completed.

In 1946, a scheme to convert the North Lake into a swimming pool was abandoned and it was to be considered for conversion into a children's boating lake and paddling pool. On 23 September 1949, however, the lake was reported as being a danger to health. When the weather was warm, the shallow lake became stagnant and the smell caused offence to people in the Municipal Maternity Home on Park Road North. On 27 January 1950, it was ordered that it should be filled in and the rough filling was reported as completed by June 1951. The work of levelling and seeding the site continued until the end of 1952.

The Sailor's Trod

This was an ancient footpath used by seamen as they walked from port to port in this northern part of Cleveland and it is mentioned in the description of the Park in the *Middlesbrough and Stockton Gazette* of 14 August 1868:

> *Several large hawthorn bushes, remains of the 'Second Sailor's Trod', a very ancient footpath, recently diverted by Act of Parliament, are next reached, and appear under widely different circumstances to what we were accustomed to see a few years ago. They are now relics of a byegone time.*

I noted earlier that it was by Act of Parliament that the total area of the Park came within the new boundaries of the Borough of Middlesbrough, a proportion having formerly been in the Township of Linthorpe. Clause 62 of the *Middlesbrough Improvement and Extension Act*, 1866, deals specifically with the question of the Sailor's Trod. In simple terms, permission was given to divert the original right of way from within the newly-established boundaries of the Park, provided that an alternative footpath was provided, further north, in its place. The Albert Park plan of

Hawthorn trees from the old Sailor's Trod, which formerly crossed the land on which the Park was laid out. Photo David Kelsey

The 'Message Tree', where passing sailors would leave notes underneath a stone between the two main branches. Photo George Ward

1875 shows that the new path lay between Park Road North and Granville Road, which is where we have Park Lane today.

The following extract from the 1866 Act gives an indication of the landscape and landownership involved in re-aligning the footpath, together with a flavour of the wording of such a document:

The Local Board may divert and permanently stop up so much of the public Footpath called 'the Second Sailor's Trod Footpath', in the Townships of Middlesbrough and Marton, as is situate between Linthorpe Road in the Township of Middlesbrough and Ormesby Beck on the East Side of the said Township of Marton, and may make and maintain in lieu of such Footpath so to be diverted and stopped up, and before the same is so stopped up, a new Footpath commencing at the North Side of a Brickyard lately belonging to Ann Outred, and agreed to be sold by her to the Local Board of the existing District, and passing thence into and through Land belonging to the Local Board, and thence into and through other Land belonging to Joseph Pease, John Pease, and Henry Pease, situate in the Township and Parish of Marton, and terminating at Ormesby Beck, situate on the East Side of the Township and Parish of Marton, and for the purpose of such diverted or new Footpath the Local Board may purchase by Agreement, and not by Compulsion, from the Owners, Lessees and occupiers of the last-mentioned Lands on the Line of such Path, so much of such Land or such Right of Way over the same as may be necessary for such new Footpath, and upon the formation of such new Footpath the old Line of Footpath shall be stopped up, and Right of Way over the same shall cease.

According to tradition, one of the hawthorn trees on the original route of the Sailor's Trod, which is now close to the Park's northern perimeter footpath, was used as a depository for messages between passing seamen, who placed them under a stone within the hollow of diverging branches. It is fascinating to think of this practice just now, as we ourselves follow that same route.

The Gymnasium

The Gymnasium was, in itself, one of the original design features of the Park in Sector 2, noted in the description of 1868, but not then in existence. There is no indication as to why its construction had been delayed, but the description of 1871 also simply refers to it as a possible addition to the amenities of the Park. Twelve years later, on 29 May 1883, the Borough Surveyor was instructed to report on gymnasia in other parks, with a view to establishing one here. Within a month, on 13th June, it was decided to proceed with the scheme, on a site to the south of the North Lake.

The Park Committee Minutes are dotted with references to a variety of accidents and it is a noteworthy fact that many of these were associated with water. A report submitted on 28 August 1883, however, reveals the dangerous nature of activities at the Gymnasium. During the previous three weeks, there were six falls from the rings and two from the horizontal bar, injuries sustained including sprained wrists and ankles, broken arms and 'damaged head and neck'.

The following description of the Gymnasium at that time, from the pen of 'A Rambler', appeared in the *Middlesbrough Daily Exchange* of 6 September 1883 and it is very enlightening:

A short distance off (from the North Lake) *there is the new gymnasium, consisting of a series of swings, a horizontal bar, and a trapeze. This form of amusement has become a great attraction to youths and boys, who crowd around the rings all day, and would be willing to extend their gymnastic performances on Sundays, if the Park Committee would allow them. To my mind, the gymnasium is the most incongruous feature I have met with in the park. It is so essentially an artificial contrivance, and forms such a focus for all the 'roughs' of the neighbourhood, that it greatly detracts from the rural simplicity which pervades nearly every other part of the park, and it is almost a pity that the Park Committee have approved it. Otherwise, there is plenty of scope in the park for amusement, for there are grounds for cricket, football, lawn tennis, and bowls, while boating and fishing can be had on the large lake.*

The writer was clearly very disapproving of the Gymnasium and, presumably, would not have been disappointed if the Committee had delayed its installation permanently. It attracted the undesirable element of the younger generation and did not fit into his overall concept of laudable amenities for the public.

At a Committee meeting held on 14 January 1884, it was ordered that the Gymnasium should be removed at once, but on 26 August of the same year the Sub-committee was instructed to consider its better management. On 18 June 1885, the Sub-committee reported that new rules of management were not needed because the Gymnasium was working well.

During the First War, the Gymnasium facilities were used for military training purposes (see Chapter Five – Wartime Activities), then on 19 July 1919, it was ordered that the swings should be removed to the Clairville Road Recreation Ground. Thereafter, the Gymnasium is not mentioned again in the Minutes.

Refreshments and Refreshment Rooms

As we have seen on more than one occasion, not all newspaper commentators were unstinting in their praises of the Park and its facilities and it was one of their number who highlighted a particular shortcoming – the lack of refreshments. He wrote in the *Middlesbrough Daily Exchange* of 10 August 1871:

Finally, a recent visit to the Park has convinced us that the one great desideratum at present is a place where refreshments can be obtained. The scorching rays of an August sun have heightened immensely, in our minds, the value of gingerbeer and kindred innoxious beverages, and we would ask what is there to prevent the Parks Committee from at once providing that thirsty cricketers and other ardent cultivators of physique should have an opportunity of slaking a thirst which at times, with the sun at 100 degrees flaring full upon them and drying every tissue of the body, is hardly to be endured.

Before any provision was made for refreshments in the Park, Mrs Cleaton, the Curator's wife, found herself in the position of having to dispense water to thirsty souls who presented themselves at her door. The first reference to a drinking fountain appears in the Park Committee Minutes of 8 August 1872 and on 29 April 1890 it was reported that the drinking fountain presented by the late John Dunning was always out of order. Six years later, a handsome fountain in memory of Henry

The early refreshment rooms, pictured in relation to the fountain. Derek Enderby Collection

The later cafe on the site of the refreshment rooms, pictured in 1982. Ken Sherwood Collection

Bolckow was presented by Hugh Gilzean-Reid, proprietor of the *North Eastern Daily Gazette*, and this is considered in Chapter Six.

Actual Refreshment Rooms were certainly in operation in the Park by 1875, being situated in the south-west corner of Sector 2. In the summer of that year, the Park Committee was considering arrangements for letting the premises to a contractor. The system appears to have been functioning most satisfactorily several seasons later, as reported in the *Middlesbrough Daily Exchange* of 18 May 1881:

> *The refreshment shelter house in the centre of the park is becoming yearly more appreciated. The tenant this year is Mr John Wake, the well-known confectioner of Newport-road. Strangers find the refreshment house a great convenience, and patronise the liberally provided buffet in increasing numbers.*

In 1884, John Wake was given permission to erect a marquee in which to serve refreshments for those involved in ice-skating on the lake. Fourteen years later, his widow took over the management of the Refreshment Rooms and of the hiring of boats.

The tenancy of the Refreshment Rooms changed hands several times over the years and in 1916 the premises were managed by Mr Angelo Rea on behalf of Messrs Tom Dent. On 18 September 1917, it was agreed that Lady Bell should have the use of the Refreshment Rooms as a Tea Garden. She, incidentally, was the compiler of the social survey of Middlesbrough entitled *At the Works*, published in 1907, and wife of Sir Hugh Bell of Bell Brothers Ironworks at Port Clarence. Subsequently, on 19 February 1918, it was decided that other premises near the boating lake should be converted into a shelter.

Ice cream proved to be a popular commodity for visitors to the Park and it is interesting to note that in 1922 Committee Members decided to report proprietors of ice cream carts for causing a nuisance at the main entrance. In any case, Rea's ice cream parlour was directly opposite the Park gates, one member of that noted family being Chris Rea, the popular singer. Just before the outbreak of the Second World War, the Parks Committee was considering plans for the provision of a new cafe, the old Tea Rooms to be converted into an old people's shelter.

Facilities for the Younger Generation
It is clear that the recreational needs of children were not high on the list of priorities in the original design concept of the Park and it is to be assumed that the younger generation simply had to make the best possible use of available open space.

On 20 August 1897, just over twenty-nine years after the Park was officially opened, the Committee decided to allocate the sum of £20 for the provision of swings for children. These were to be erected at the east end of the lower Archery Bank, 'as this is a place where a large number of children frequent'. In September 1901, there is a further reference to swings, which were to be placed opposite the lower lodge and near the Archery Ground. More swings were erected in 1909 and it is interesting to note that in June 1914 the police complained that adults were using them.

The Miniature Railway
On 24 May 1946, the Parks Committee considered a request from the Tees-Side Society of Model and Experimental Engineers 'regarding the possibility of

permission being granted for the Society to lay a miniature passenger carrying track in the Albert Park or other suitable place'. The scheme was approved in July 1946, the site allocated being between the main walk and the Bell Hill. This proved to be a very popular feature in the Park, a model station being added in 1961 and the track being extended two years later. The railway continued in use until 1988, when fire destroyed the premises in which the rolling stock and equipment were stored.

In 1991, plans from a private individual to resurrect the railway were considered by the Council, but they did not come to fruition, the suggested site having already been earmarked for an integrated play area. Ten years later, however, it is interesting to note that, even though the Restoration Master Plan does not incorporate a scheme for a railway, independent discussions have taken place with the Great Northern Steam Company, with a view to costing ideas and proposals.

The Modern Playground

The new facilities for the integrated play area were officially opened in June 1994, being the culmination of many months of work to create a playground where both

The Integrated Play Area, showing the ground plan and the geometrical climbing frame.
Photo Tansee Cartwright

The geometrical climbing frame. Photo Tansee Cartwright

able-bodied and disabled children can play together. It has certainly proved to be a popular attraction for youngsters, a fact which has been proved on many occasions by our grandchildren. Laura's favourite apparatus is the geometrically-designed climbing frame while noisy young Andrew particularly enjoys slamming the metal gate and running away.

Local residents, schools and disabled groups were actively involved in choosing the equipment which, where possible, was to be accessible for wheelchair users. Tactile textured paving has been used to edge the paths, which helps those who are visually impaired to find their way around the play area, warning them of surface changes from sand to path or path to bark.

Brightly coloured and contrasting paintwork helps the visually handicapped to distinguish between the different pieces of equipment and gives the whole area a colourful appearance. With safety in mind, dog grills and gates are provided at each entrance. It is, however, possible to bring guide dogs on to the site.

An unusual and interesting feature at the south gate is the metal braille map which was created by local artist Steven Poulton. Incorporating ideas put forward by pupils from the Visually Impaired unit at Ormesby School, it helps children to find their way around in the play area.

Toilets

The first example of twenty-first century architecture which we encounter on our tour of the Park is the toilet block to the west of the play area. This, in itself, represents the ultimate achievement in the on-going saga of catering for the most basic needs of Park visitors.

On 4 March 1869, more than six months after the official opening of the Park, the Surveyor was instructed to obtain four urinals and to have them fixed at once. On 10 April of the same year, it was ordered that another urinal and a water closet were to be placed at the south end of the Upper Lake and that a urinal was to be placed near the proposed North Lake.

It was reported on 28 April 1885 that, by that time, there was a total of fourteen

Toilets old and new, with the 1958 block in the foreground and the 2001 replacement block behind, under construction. Photo Tansee Cartwright

privies in the Park, six of which were for ladies and eight for gentlemen, the latter also having access to four urinals. The Curator emphasised the fact that there was no water laid on to any of these facilities and 'all has to be carried'. He asked that they should all be cleaned out daily before 6.00 a.m. and it was agreed that a Park workman should be paid an additional five shillings per week for the privilege of starting this task at 4.00 a.m. In later years, the practice was to use a bucket of ash to cover the contents of the toilet after each visit.

We are given an intriguing insight into the actual structure of these dry closets in a Ken Sherwood anecdote about a practical joke which some of the lads played on an older colleague – Laurie Stobbs. The cruelty of the prank was based on the fact that the Depot yard was then being plagued by rats from the nearby Cannon Lake. During the course of one of Laurie's visits to the toilet, the door which gave access for the removal of the pan was quietly opened and the revealed nether region was tickled with the rabbit's tail on a stick which was used in the process of pollenating. The horrified victim leapt out of the cubicle and announced that he had just been touched by a rat!

Over the years, Committee Minutes reveal that new toilets were provided in various parts of the Park and that arrangements were made to up-grade them as necessary. The present site in Sector 2 was first used for toilets in association with the nearby Refreshment Rooms, their replacement by the recently-demolished block being ordered in 1958.

At the time of the Restoration Project survey, some four decades later, this block was found to be 'an unacceptably poor quality facility, physically and visually' and its fate was sealed. Before actual demolition was effected, however, the elements took a hand, a very strong wind blowing down a nearby oak tree, which fell directly on to the toilet building. Rather than saving the contractors a job, this incident created another and the tree had to be cleared. It had sheared off near the base and, rather than being rotten inside, it was revealed that the trunk was weak because the annual bark rings had separated, rather like a series of tubes placed one inside the other.

The impressive replacement block, the design of which is in keeping with the new Visitor Centre in Sector 3, offers separate male and female facilities, each with units for the disabled, and there is also family/baby-changing accommodation. The new building was completed in December 2001 and is set slightly further back from the East Walk than its predecessor and it will be partially screened from it by shrubs. The Master Plan costing for this scheme was £82,200.

The East End of the Park

The Stone Steps
Access to the east end of the Park from the Chestnut Avenue is by means of an imposing flight of stone steps which is one of the extant original features of the William Barratt design. He would have seen their like while visiting other parks and his use of Halifax stone is indicative of local contacts from his home base in

The stone steps leading from the Chestnut Avenue to the Lower Lake. Photo George Ward

Wakefield. An interesting description of the steps was recorded in the account of the official opening of the Park:

> *The main walk is continued from the opposite side of this promenade for a further distance of 1,000 feet, when it is terminated by a handsome flight of stone steps, leading to the lower lake. The walk is planted on each side with three varieties of horse chestnuts, and the steps are somewhat remarkable in their way. Each step is 12 feet long, 18 inches broad, and 6 inches deep, and is one solid block, cut from stone hewn in the neighbourhood of Halifax. Upon each side of the steps is a low stone coping and at the corners are pillars. These pillars are surmounted by vases, and these give the steps a very complete appearance.*

The condition of these steps has deteriorated over time and they are earmarked for restoration, in conjunction with the general improvement of pedestrian movement in that area.

The East Lodge and Former Cottages

On leaving Sector 2 by means of these steps, and before exploring Sector 3, we will consider the principal features at the east end of the Park, commencing at its northern extremity with the East Lodge.

By virtue of the fact that it was not the Curator's residence, the East Lodge receives little attention in the Park Committee Minutes. In itself, it is, in fact, a more imposing building, but there is no reference to it in the Department of the Environment *List of Buildings of Special Architectural or Historical Interest* (1988). Its

The East Lodge, erected in 1871 and still in use as residences. Photo Tansee Cartwright

tenancy and maintenance are occasionally mentioned to Committee as a matter of routine and it is interesting to note that occupants over the years included Police Officers and their families.

Originally, there were two cottages in the area of the East Lodge and it would appear that these were in existence when the land for the Park was actually purchased, being mentioned in passing in the legal documents dealing with that transaction. It is not clear, however, as to when these properties were actually acquired by the Corporation and it seems possible that the sitting tenants continued as occupants.

The cottages were clearly of topical interest at the monthly Council Meeting on 11 February 1873, when the Borough Accountant was asked to comment on their cost. He said that this had been between £600 and £700 each, an outlay which was expected to be recovered in rents within thirteen or fourteen years. There is no record of the eventual demise of the cottages, but Ken Sherwood refers to them as still being there in 1969.

The Lower Lake

The most outstanding feature at the east end of the park is the one remaining lake, which has been extremely popular from the very beginning. At the time of the official opening of the Park, it was described thus:

> *At the end of the Swiss walk, the lower lake is reached, and taking a turn to the left, and pausing upon a bridge at the northern extremity, the waterfall, nearly 30 feet wide, and about five feet in depth, will be seen to advantage, and also the lake itself. From this point, nearly the whole length is seen, and the curving banks form a very rural scene. There are two small islands near to the western side, and a*

The central island in the Lower Lake, removed in 2001 for replacement by a water-jet feature as part of the Restoration Plan. Photo Tansee Cartwright

large one in the centre, rising to a height of fifteen feet. It will be planted round with trees, and surmounted at the top by a quaint-looking house, intended for the accommodation of the swans, ducks and other waterfowl that may disport themselves upon the lake, the edges of which have been made of stone, for the purpose of keeping the water clean.

Bridges

The 1868 description of the Park mentions not only a bridge at the north end of the Lower Lake, but also another at the south end. The Park Committee Minutes of 8 July 1875 refer to a proposed new cast iron bridge for the ornamental lake and this was reported as fixed by 3 May 1876. On 26 September 1882, there was a reference to a Bow String Bridge on the Lower Lake, while a footbridge over Marton West Beck, running along the eastern boundary of the Park, was planned in April 1890, to give access to the new east gate.

The Waterfall

The waterfall referred to in 1868 was one of the more unusual features of the Park and this was a matter for Committee consideration two decades later, when, on 28 February 1888, it was highlighted in the Curator's report:

Sirs, – LOW LAKE. – Last Autumn you raised the water fall 8 inches which makes the North-east side of the Lake 4 feet 4 inches deep. At the Council Meeting held December 13th 1887, it was considered not to be safe for skating upon, therefore you ordered me to lower the water about 18 inches. I did so, now 4 feet 4 inches of water will not be any too deep for Boating upon. Please order the depth you wish me to keep the water to.

The Committee ordered that no alteration should be made to the depth of the water and it is interesting to note that the issue had been raised at Council in the context of the popular pastime of ice skating.

Ice Skating

It might be imagined that this activity would simply have been a casual, opportunist pastime during the winter season, but this was not, in fact, the case. Special care was taken with the preparation of the surface of the ice and, when necessary, extra men were drafted in to undertake the work. On one occasion (in December 1925), overtime payment was actually authorised when this work was in hand. It was a matter of concern to the Park Committee that the ice should not be used until it was ready and on 28 December 1880 they agreed to put in a request for Police supervision.

As we saw earlier, the presence of skaters was regarded as a source of income by John Wake, the proprietor of the Refreshment Rooms, who, in November 1884 was given permission to erect a marquee near the lake for the benefit of skaters. To a lesser degree, the Committee itself saw an opportunity for gaining income and on 23 December 1878 they had ordered that a box should be placed near the lake for subscriptions from skaters. It would appear that access for skating was only available according to the severity of the weather and when officially stated. The sport was still

Ice-skating on the Lower Lake. Ken Sherwood Collection

taken seriously in 1946, being referred to on 18 January, when the Parks Superintendent was authorised to use floodlights at the lake.

Just as a little aside, it is interesting to note that on 28 December 1880, it was agreed that shinty could be played on the ice.

Maintenance

The actual work of maintaining the Lower Lake involved periodic draining and cleaning, which has always been a difficult operation. This fact is underlined in a report presented to Committee by the Acting Park Curator on 20 February 1923:

> CLEANING OUT LARGE LAKE
>
> *This work has been started and we have made the following progress: The water has been drained from the Lake and all the Fish have been caught and temporarily transferred to the narrow inlet at the South End of the Lake, which we dammed up for the purpose of preserving them until the work has been completed.*
>
> *To the best of my knowledge the Fish are chiefly Roach of which there are many hundreds. There is a great amount of mud and other debris which we have commenced to remove. Owing to the constant rains, there is a continual flow from the land drains (which of course we cannot avoid). This makes the work more difficult on account of the very wet condition of the mud. The work must be completed and the Lake refilled in readiness for the Boating Season, which commences on Good Friday, 30 March. Failing this it would mean a loss of income on the Boats.*

Some indication of the amount of effort involved in this operation may be gained from a further report which was presented to Committee on 20 March 1923:

RE LARGE LAKE

As the Committee are aware we are engaged in the Cleaning out of the Lake. We have removed a good portion of the mud from the end near the Boat landing, thoroughly cleaned out the Boat House, also the extreme end around the outlet of Lake, these being the most necessary places. Of course, it would be impossible to clean the whole area of the Lake before warmer weather commences owing to the late start we made.

We are busy with the rebuilding of slag around the Islands and banks of the Lake, which will be completed in the course of a day or two. It is then intended to fill up again, in readiness for the Boating Season, which will commence on Good Friday, 30 March.

The flow from the beck is very slow and should the dry weather continue, it will take it all its time to fill up the Lake by that date.

The lake was cleaned again in 1936, but its actual water quality proved to be a problem in the very hot Summer of 1952, when 200 fish were found to have died through lack of oxygen. At the Committee Meeting held on 19 September, the Borough Engineer presented the following report, clearly indicating the difficulties involved in achieving a balance between the needs of the lake, the availability of water supply and the safety of the public:

BOATING LAKE – PROVISION OF CONSTANT WATER SUPPLY – As instructed by your Committee on 4 July 1952, the possibility of providing a constant water supply from the Marton West Beck to the lake has been investigated.

Following the deepening and widening of the beck as a flood prevention scheme, which prevented any natural flow into the lake, a feed was provided to the Park from an existing drain which discharged ground water from the old brick field pond in the Cumberland Road area. Since the recent building operations this feed has dried up.

Whilst the beck could be dammed at a point opposite the junction of York Road and Cumberland Road and water diverted to the lake, observations taken during August of the summer flow in the stream indicate that the discharge is very small. If all this could be used it would require a period of flow of at least two months to effect a change of water in the lake.

After allowing for evaporation and leakages this source of feed is almost negligible and would have little material value in providing a fresh water supply during the summer months. The risk to children playing in or near the beck if such a dam were constructed must not be overlooked nor the greater risk due to such obstruction in the beck, to the efficiency of the flood prevention scheme for which the culvert was constructed.

In 1946 a feed pipe was laid to the paddling pool from the water main in Park Road South to provide for periodic flushing of the paddling pool during the summer months. Whilst this feed could be extended to the Park lake, it is questionable whether the Tees Valley Water Board would permit of the use of water for this purpose during the summer months. In any event the cost of water to effect one complete change of the lake would be costly.

If the paddling pool is to be abandoned, the existing feed pipe at the head of the pool would require extending to the lake. It is estimated that this will cost £350.

The Committee ordered that the paddling pool should be permanently closed and that the feed pipe should be extended as recommended. The matter was then to be given further consideration.

On 18 February 1955, it was ordered that authority should be given for carrying out the recommendations of the Borough Engineer in the following report:

It is understood from the Tees Valley Water Board that they are now able to supply sufficient water for renewal of the lake water, if taken at night. On this basis it would take a period of about one month to renew the whole quantity of water in the lake.

The existing water pipe discharges into the paddling pool, and it is now proposed to lay 6in. stoneware pipe along the side of the pool, connecting with an existing drain which will discharge the water into the lake. If agreed, this work can be done before the end of the financial year. The estimated cost is £200, and an amount of £350 is included in the current Annual Estimates.

A great deal of valuable information relating to the maintenance of the Lower Lake has obviously been gleaned from Committee Minutes, but I have been particularly impressed by a first-hand account of the actual process of cleaning it in September 1969, which was passed on by Ken Sherwood.

The first requisite was to remove all of the fish from the lake and this involved the use of an electric stun-gun, powered by a generator which was taken out by means of a boat. Once the fish were immobilised, there being 32,000 in total, they were removed and transported to other lakes throughout Teesside. Those which were

Stunning the fish before emptying the Lower Lake for cleaning in 1969. Ken Sherwood Collection

kept at Stewart Park were to be brought home in due course. There was also a number of very large eels, in the region of a metre in length, and these had to be moved in dustbins. They were, however, long enough to stand on their tails and make their escape by jumping out and scurrying away. One of the men had to dip his hands into a bucket of sharp sand, run after them and pop them back into the dustbins, with a lad on stand-by to hold the lid down. On one occasion, a passer-by asked if he could have an eel and one of them was duly killed for him. Two days later, he returned with a jar of jellied eel for Ken, but he did not believe in eating anything which had come out of that lake!

It took two six-inch pumps a full week of non-stop operation to drain the lake and the process of clearing the slurry from its bed began in the following month with the laying of stone paths from the shore into the lake, on which dumpers were run for ease of loading. This was effected by means of a crane, with a bucket which scooped up the slurry after the latter had been pushed to the side of the lake by a bulldozer. As we saw earlier, the slurry was then dumped at the Bell Hill site. Unfortunately, the bulldozer became embedded into the sediment and somebody remarked that, at a valuation of some £20,000, it could well become the most expensive man-made island in the lake. Eventually, it was pulled clear by other bulldozers and replaced by a huge wide-tracked machine which was specially designed for working in swamps. This saved the day and Ken recorded in his work diary that the work was finished by 14 November. Exactly five months later, on 14 April 1970, the fish at Stewart Park had another stunning experience and they were brought back home.

The Paddling Pool and Sand Pit
It is evident that the water supply to the Lower Lake was closely linked to that of the paddling pool and that the fate of the latter depended upon what was deemed to be best for the former. It is, however, interesting to see that, even though the paddling pool was ordered to be permanently closed in 1952, it was still being referred to three years later.

For the actual origins of the paddling pool, in association with a sand pit, the Committee Minutes take us back to the year 1925. Before dipping into those, however, it is worth noting that a separate scheme for a sand pit had been put forward as early as 18 July 1911, at an estimated cost of £45 to £50. At the request of the Committee Chairman, the Curator and Borough Engineer had looked at a suitable site in Sector 2, between the North Lake and the former Archery Ground. The upshot, however, was a Committee decision that the matter should not be pursued at that time.

On 14 July 1925, the Curator reported as follows:

The new Paddling Pool and Sand Pit being completed, was opened on 27 June and is already a great success, hundreds of children having been attracted to it, spending the whole of their time paddling and playing in the Sand Pit. By providing such facilities for children, it will keep many of them away from the more important parts of the Park, which should mean less damage to Trees, Shrubs, etc.

I must draw the Committee's attention to a danger which has arisen since the construction of the paddling pool. The narrow stretch of water which continues from the weir of the pool to the Boathouse (some 50 yards in length) should either be fenced in, or filled up with slag and faced over with concrete. The Chairman and I have talked this matter over, and he agrees that something should be done, as this part of the Lake is deep and very dangerous. Perhaps the Committee will visit this place and draw their own conclusion.

Ten days later, on 24 July, Committee Members did, in fact, visit the Park, in order to inspect a number of sites, including the area of the paddling pool, and it was ordered that a notice should be posted at the watercourse linking the pool to the lake in order to warn children of the danger of entering the water there. It was also ordered that a wire guard should be fitted over the spiked railings near the paddling pool and that a notice should be displayed as a warning against allowing dogs to enter the pool. As a means of avoiding accidents, the introduction of glass bottles into the pool itself was to be forbidden.

On 15 September, Committee Members were informed that, in spite of all their best efforts, there had actually been an accident in the watercourse between the lake and paddling pool just four days after their visit. A two-year-old named Mary Wall had fallen into the water and was rescued by a Park labourer who just happened to be working in that area. He subsequently took her back home, and the fact that the accident had occurred at 6.30 in the evening makes one wonder about parental care. Following this accident, the watercourse was temporarily fenced off and it was recommended that this arrangement should be made permanent in order to stop children actually reaching the danger area.

Water quality in the paddling pool was another matter of concern and it was improved in 1932, when the Lower Lake itself was linked to a supply of fresh water. Furthermore, in 1946 special arrangements were made for the pool itself to be linked directly to the water main by means of a new pipe of its own.

In spite of the official ban on taking bottles to the paddling pool, the practice continued into the War years and Ken Sherwood remembers being involved in draining the pool in order to clear out all the broken glass. This, however, was a popular job for him and his mates, since they very often retrieved coins which had been lost by children using the pool. It was also a common occurrence for employees to find money when digging turves in the Park where people had been sitting on the grass. On one occasion, Ken himself found half a crown ($12\frac{1}{2}$p), which was quite a sum in those days.

Over the years, numerous accidents involving young children have occurred not only in the paddling pool but also in the lakes themselves and there are reports of heroic rescues by adults in that context as well. One of these involved a perambulator, which had run away down a sloping path and into the water. The rescuers were always commended for their bravery but, interestingly enough, some of them felt that this was not all that was to be expected. They did not seem to mind putting themselves at risk in the best interests of the youngsters, but insisted on claiming compensation in relation to damage to clothing.

Committee Minutes reveal very few references to the sand pit in isolation from the paddling pool. It does, however, emerge that in 1955 the Superintendent reported that it was in a dirty condition, being difficult to maintain because it was so large. He recommended that it should be either done away with altogether or reduced in size. It was decided that it should be retained but made smaller in order to be more hygienic and more convenient to maintain. The original size of sixty-one feet by fifty-one feet was to be reduced to twenty-one feet by fifty-one feet, at an estimated cost of £75. The reclaimed area was to be used as an extension to the playground.

Boats and Boating

The Lower Lake has, over the years, also been referred to as the Large Lake or the East Lake, but it is much better known as the Boating Lake. For almost the first decade after the opening of the Park, however, not a single boat had been available for hire on the lake.

On 19 June 1876, the Park Committee agreed to approach Henry Bolckow on the matter of the best way of acquiring boats, but Councillor Livingstone decided to take the initiative himself. His gift of a boat was gratefully accepted at the Committee meeting held on 2 August 1876, when it was also agreed that another boat should be purchased for not more than £15. On 6 February 1878, it was decided that a landing stage for the boats should be erected at a cost not exceeding £5.

Committee Minutes show how other boats were purchased and how popular they were with visitors. By 25 May 1880, four craft were in use and the Curator presented the following report on that occasion:

PARK BOATS
The number of persons using these Boats from 21 April to 20 May 1880 are as under:

		£	s	d
Onward	147	2	3	0
Forward	139	1	18	9
Water Lily	109	1	9	6
Livingstone	21	1	9	0
	416	£6	10	3

Boating facilities on the Lower Lake are referred to by the commentators in the *Middlesbrough Daily Exchange* of 18 May 1881 and 6 September 1883. They each give an interesting insight into the financial side of hiring the boats:

> *There are now several boats on the lake, and in the summer season these are more and more in request. They are let out at the rate of 1s. per hour, but when they are occupied by more than four persons at a time threepence per head extra is charged. The smaller boats are in the greatest request, and on holidays especially are kept busily employed.*
>
> *Otherwise, there is plenty of scope in the park for amusement, for there are grounds for cricket, football, lawn tennis, and bowls, while boating and fishing can be had on the large lake. The boating is popular, and earns a modest little revenue for the committee.*

On 17 February 1885, it was decided to purchase a new punt for £5 5s 0d and on 28 February 1893 an Indian canoe was made available by Mr D McArthur. On 27

Rowing boats and the old boat house. Derek Enderby Collection

January 1891, plans were approved for a boat house in which the craft could be stored and on 27 April 1897 it was reported that a new landing stage had been completed.

Committee Minutes reveal the progression of repairing and replacing the boats over the years and 20 November 1936 saw the recommendation to construct a new boat house for £350. On 13 December 1940, just over a year after the outbreak of the Second World War, the Parks Superintendent was authorised to make the boats available for use in any emergency situation.

Ken Sherwood recalls that one of the winter jobs in the Park at this time was that of producing planks from the felled trees, for which large bench saws were hired and set up in the Depot yard. George Holmes, a retired boat-builder, had joined the staff

One of the rowing boats, believed to be original Victorian, before removal for restoration in 2001. Photo Tansee Cartwright

The boat house of 1957 and its replacement of 2001. Photos George Ward and Tansee Cartwright

and he would supervise the cutting of planks to the exact size which he required. These were then stacked in his drying shed and used the following year for the construction and repair of rowing boats. George was a skilled craftsman, assisted by Frank Verrill of Hartlepool, and their work represented the careful use of the Park's resources.

The first Minutes reference to a motor boat appears on 7 September 1951, when it was reported that a borrowed craft had proved to be very popular. It had been used by 819 people over a twenty-four-day period, with an income of £40 9s 0d, and it was decided to purchase the boat for £175. Two more motor boats were acquired in the following year and this was the beginning of a small fleet of such craft, which evolved during the 1950s.

In order to improve services for the public, the provision of a new boat house was recommended to Committee in March 1957. The sum of £200 had been allocated for this work and it was in use by early August. On 20 September, the Superintendent reported that it had already led to improvement in the turn-round of boats, even during busy periods, and he added that the new loudspeaker equipment was also very beneficial. Up to that time, boats in need of repair had been transported to Stewart Park, but the new building made it possible for such maintenance to be carried out on site.

The Committee Minutes have not revealed any further references to the boat house, which was felt by the Restoration Consultants to be an unattractive building. It was, therefore, decided to replace this building on the west side of the lake with a new one on a site at the south end of the lake which had been used for an even earlier boat house. Completion of the new building was scheduled for January 2002, with a concrete ramp from the lake facilitating the movement of the boats for both storage and repair, while direct public access to the boats will be provided by means of a new jetty. The Master Plan costing for this scheme was £51,100.

It had become evident that the boats themselves were in need of refurbishment and arrangements were made for this work to be undertaken as one of the projects which were identified within the Restoration Plan as being suitable for the involvement of community-based groups. Using the manpower resources of HM Prison Deerbolt, the six original Victorian rowing boats from the present fleet of twelve craft have been repaired. They were transported to that establishment on 16 October 2001 by a team from the Territorial Army.

It can be noted in passing that local Probation Services and Prison establishments personnel have also been enlisted to help with the painting and refurbishment of railings; the removal of dog runs; the demolition of the toilet block; the reinstatement of the Sunk Walk, and aspects of planting and walkway works.

Fishing and Fish

In considering problems relating to the maintenance of the Lower Lake, we saw the serious effect of poor oxygenation on the fish population itself, which would clearly be a matter of great concern both to the Park authorities and to local anglers.

Fishing was a popular pastime in the Park from the outset, an eventuality which had been anticipated in the original bye-laws of 1868. Clause 4 stated that no fish could be taken without written permission and the question of licences appears in the

Committee Minutes as early as 15 June 1869. It was clearly an offence to breach the regulations and in July of the same year former Councillor Thomas Brentnall was found to be at fault. Having been caught red-handed, he was duly challenged and became verbally abusive.

Members of the Middlesbrough Angling Club were regular users of the Park's facilities and they kept a close eye on the Council's charges for licences over the years. Reference is made to the formation of a new Club in 1956 and arrangements were made for an Angling Competition in September 1962.

The Park's fish stock was periodically monitored and replenished as necessary. On 9 November 1878, it was ordered that Mr Hustler of Acklam Hall was to be thanked for providing fish from his lake for the stocking of the new North Lake. From 1875, the Minutes reveal references to the actual breeding of fish and to the spawning beds. In this context, and with reference to the actual breeds of fish in the Park, the following newspaper accounts are of interest:

> *In former years a great deal of fish-breeding – or pisciculture, as it is scientifically called – went on at the park under the careful superintendence of Mr Alderman Todd, but this year the lower lake is stocked, and it is not felt necessary to add to the numbers of the finny tribes that inhabit its waters. These consist of trout, grayling, and perch, and the trout, we are told, are very fine, and some of them of large size. A special spawning place is provided for the fish up stream at the head of the lake, and during last spawning season those interested in the gentle art which Isaac Walton loved so well were afforded much entertainment by watching the fishes come up, in a kind of bridal procession, two and two, to the spawning beds. (Middlesbrough Daily Exchange of 18 May 1881)*
>
> *Fishing is more extensive than when first the licenses were granted. In the large lake some well-grown perch can be obtained, and also a few grayling, but not many*

New fishing platforms on the east side of the lake, after it had been drained, and with the new Visitor Centre under construction. Photo Tansee Cartwright

trout. In the north lake, where fishing with ground-bait is allowed, some fine eels have lately been caught. (Middlesbrough Daily Exchange of 6 September 1883)

The significance of fishing has been acknowledged within the Restoration Plan proposals, Albert Park being the only venue for angling in the town which is available to all members of the public. It was decided that seven new fishing platforms would be provided on the east side of the lake, each of which will be accessible to both able and disabled anglers. The Master Plan costing for this scheme was £8,900.

The physical work of restoring the lake involves the removal of all fish stock, which was effected through netting as opposed to stunning. The fish were moved to Hemlington Lake and they will be replaced after the completion of the project. In line with advice received from Environment Agency Fisheries Officers, the opportunity is to be taken to adjust the balance of the fish stock, with a view to removing such species as bream and carp, which are detrimental to the ecology of the lake.

The Birds of the Park
The original fish were imported to the Park lakes, but the lakes in themselves have always been home for waterfowl, specimens noted in the late nineteenth century including Black Hambros, Decoy, Golden-headed and Red-headed Divers, Egyptian Goose, Muscovy, Pintail, Sheldrake, Swan, Widgeon and Wild Duck.

Feeding the ducks before the Lower Lake was railed off. Ken Sherwood Collection

The temporary pond which was created in 2001 for wildfowl after the draining of the Lower Lake. Photo George Ward

The Park Committee Minutes of 1894 reveal interesting details about Egyptian Geese which were owned by P.C.Douglas Morrison, the tenant of the Park's East Lodge. In May, he offered a pair of March-born goslings which he had bred himself and the gift was gratefully accepted. The Chairman was asked to enquire about the possibility of purchasing the parents. A month later, it was reported that the goslings had been received and were doing well, and that their parents had been purchased for the sum of £2 10s.

On the broader subject of birdlife, it is very interesting to note that in May and July 1912, the Curator reported to Committee that the following birds had been noted in the Park:

Blackbird	Hawfinch	Robin	Tit, Great
Blackcap	Housemartin	Rook	Tit, Long-tailed
Bramble Finch	Jackdaw	Snipe	Tree Creeper
Bullfinch	Kingfisher	Sparrow	Wagtail, Pied
Chaffinch	Lark, Sky	Sparrow, Hedge	Wagtail, Yellow
Chiffchaff	Lark, Tit	Sparrowhawk	Whitethroat
Cormorant	Linnet	Starling	Woodcock
Cuckoo	Owl, Tawny	Swallow	Woodpecker
Fieldfare	Partridge	Swift	Wren, Golden-crested
Goldfinch	Pheasant	Thrush, Missal	Wren, Jennie
Grebe, Little	Redpole	Thrush, Song	Wren, Willow
Greenfinch	Redstart	Tit, Blue	Yellow Hammer

There was no question of the birdlife of the Park being taken for granted by the Committee and on occasion members asked the Curator to make sure that the birds did not go short of seeds and water during the winter months.

Over time, Nature has allowed wildfowl stock to flourish and the Restoration

Consultants' survey indicated that the level was excessive, giving rise to management problems. Measures are therefore to be taken for the provision of fencing and mesh barriers in order to discourage the birds from encroaching upon areas of new planting. During the course of the remedial works on the lake, a temporary pond was created by volunteers, south-west of the pitch and putt area in Sector 2, so that wildfowl would not be completely deprived of an area of water.

Swimming

Clause 5 of the 1868 bye-laws placed a ban on bathing in the Park lakes and this was further endorsed on 19 June 1876, when the Park Committee issued a specific order to that effect. On special occasions, however, exceptions were made to this general ruling. In June 1902, for example, Professor Tom Hatfield, Superintendent of

Park visitors were left in no doubt about the possibility of having a dip in the Lower Lake.
Middlesbrough Reference Library

Jack Hatfield poses proudly with a fine array of his swimming trophies. Jack Hatfield Jr. Collection

Middlesbrough Swimming Baths, was able to organise a Grand Water Carnival in the lake as part of the celebrations marking the Coronation of His Majesty King Edward VII. On that occasion, he was assisted by his two sons, Tom and Jack.

Jack Hatfield was to become the most famous figure in the annals of swimming in Middlesbrough, being raised in the town after being born in Great Ayton in 1893. On 13 July 1920, the Park Committee decided that he should be allowed to train in the Lower Lake in preparation for swimming championships to be held in London. He was involved in the Antwerp Olympic Games of the same year and in 1928, when he competed in the Amsterdam Olympics, he was again allowed to train in the Park.

Having been Champion of England at the age of eighteen, Jack had also competed in the 1912 Olympics in Stockholm and in Paris in 1924. In the Summer of 1928, he was given permission to stage a swimming gala in the Park, where, as an Olympic silver and bronze medal-winner, he was very well received.

Jack's training sessions were in themselves another source of great interest to crowds of unemployed onlookers, that being the time of the Great Depression. Jack Junior has told me that his Dad recalled how he would swim around the islands on a variety of courses, so that he was not going head-on into the mud churned up from the bed of the lake during his previous circuit. On completing his swim, he would wrap himself in a robe before making his way to the Middlesbrough Baths, where he would have a good wash down in order to remove all the mud and grime from the lake.

Jack Hatfield appears to have been one of the few Middlesbrough residents to enter the Lower Lake with an official blessing, but, tragically, its waters have proved to be of interest to numerous others over the years.

Professor Tom Hatfield, Superintendent of Middlesbrough Swimming Baths, with sons Jack and Tom in 1902. Jack Hatfield Jr. Collection

Suicide Attempted and Achieved

In my own experience, visits to Albert Park have always been associated with enjoyable activities and it is upsetting to think of those individuals who had every intention of making one particular visit their last. Between 1927 and 1940, Committee Minutes reveal details of five local residents who were involved in incidents at the Lower Lake. I will let the reports of the Curator or Superintendent speak for themselves, while amending the names and addresses of the individuals involved.

Tuesday 20 September 1927

On the morning of the 27 July inst, Ada ... (22), of ... Marton Road, attempted suicide in the large lake at the Park, but luckily a young boy, who was passing on his bicycle at the time, saw the woman in the water and got in for her, and with the assistance of Charles Bould, of Grove Hill, who then came on the scene, succeeded in pulling her out. The young man then disappeared and Bould took the woman home. This occurred just before seven o'clock in the morning, and was reported to me by Thomas Wallis, one of the Park workmen, who happened to be passing on his way to work at the time.

I informed the police who at once took the matter in hand and the young woman was sent to Holgate for a few days for medical observation and then appearing before the Court later, was bound over in the sum of ten pounds for two years.

Wednesday 11 September 1929

On the 9th ultimo, a woman named Margaret... of... School Croft attempted suicide by throwing herself into the large lake in Albert Park. Fortunately some boys who were near at the time caught hold of her, raised the alarm, and the Boatman pulled her out, and she was removed to Holgate.

Friday 14 July 1939

I also have to report that on the 5th instant at about 10.00 p.m. a young woman (32 years of age) attempted to commit suicide in the big lake at the Albert Park, this occurring just before the gate was locked at the North East corner, close by the end of the lake where this happened.

Luckily, two fishermen – Mr E Bregazzi of 30 Athol Street, and Mr A Clare of 85 Park Lane – were just leaving this particular part of the lake when they heard a splash and saw the woman in the water.

Mr Bregazzi immediately went into the lake and with the help of his companion and one of the Park gardeners from the lodge near (sic) *who had come on the scene, dragged the woman out and took her to the lodge, where she recovered after some attention.*

The Police were, of course, notified at once and she was removed by ambulance to Holgate and later to St Luke's Hospital being, I understand, certified insane.

A day or two later Mr Bregazzi called to see me and complained that he had ruined his clothes and he did not think that cleaning and pressing would be any use as they were in a most abominable state.

I might add that the lake is nearly five feet deep where Mr Bregazzi went in and he informed me he was up to his armpits in the water and being the outlet end of the lake there is always quite a lot of mud and debris here.

Will the Committee please give their instructions.

Ordered as follows:

1. That the best thanks of the Committee be tendered to Mr Bregazzi for his efforts in getting the young woman out of the east lake at the Albert Park on the 5th July 1939.

2. That the Chairman and the Town Clerk be authorised to deal with the question of granting suitable recognition to Mr Bregazzi.

27 September 1939

I also report that at 8 a.m. on the 14th instant a woman (about 60 years of age), attempted suicide in the big lake in the Albert Park.

On the morning in question, the foreman gardener was passing along the side of the lake when he saw a woman in the water near the boat landing. He summoned the ambulance at once and this person was removed to Holgate.

I understand that she recovered fairly quickly and was later removed to her home.

Friday 22 November 1940

BODY IN PARK LAKE (SUSPECTED SUICIDE CASE)

The Town Clerk submitted verbally a report from the Parks Superintendent on the

*finding on the morning of the 23rd October last, of the body of a woman in the
Albert Park big lake.*

As well as highlighting the tragic side of the lives of five local women, these extracts
also indicate various aspects of the life of the Park itself, together with general
procedures in relation to attempted suicide.

It is evident that Park employees started work at a very early hour and that visitors
(fishermen at least) stayed until closing time. As we saw earlier, the East Lodge was
used as a residence by Park staff other than the Curator, and in 1939 the tenant was
a gardener.

In each of the four cases of attempted suicide, there was somebody available to
rescue the would-be victim and one wonders if each one may have been uttering a
cry for help. The Curator or Superintendent was obliged to report each such incident
to the Police and the individual concerned was then taken to the Holgate Hospital (at
Ayresome) for medical attention. This establishment, incidentally, had originally
been Middlesbrough's Victorian workhouse.

Restoration and Development

As a result of the survey carried out in preparation for the Heritage Lottery bid, it was
decided that the Lower Lake was visually unattractive, that the water quality was poor
and, consequently, smelly. The lake edge was in a poor condition, as was the
vegetation, particularly on the three islands. Access for fishing needed to be
improved and the user survey highlighted a low opinion of boating facilities.

The Consultants' Stage Two Submission Document contains a larger section of
proposals on the Lower Lake than on any other feature of the Park. The following is
a brief summary of the major elements within the proposals:

- Provision of a mains top-up water supply, as a source of clean water.
- Removal of sediment from the bed of the lake to improve water quality.
- Installation of an aeration system to maintain water quality.
- Removal of the central island and introduction of a water jet, as a more dramatic
  focal point to the lake.
- Full reconstruction of the edges of the lake and the two remaining islands, with
  the restoration of the original style of stone edging and vegetation.
- Replacement of the large concrete and stone spillway outlet at the north end of the
  lake with a simple overflow system.
- The provision of heritage-style lighting columns along the lakeside footpath.

As we saw earlier, the Restoration Master Plan took account of the fact that general
improvements to the drainage of the Park were essential, and this is reflected in
works at the lake, with flood alleviation measures being undertaken in January 2002.
In the past, heavy rain has caused annual problems both within the Park, the Marton
West Beck and the adjacent area beyond the actual Park boundary. As a means of
dealing with excess water, a specially-landscaped area north of the lake was ear-
marked for the creation of a holding basin. After the completion of this work, the lake
itself is to be re-filled by Northumbrian Water, a process which is expected to take up
to a week. The water will then take some time to settle into a natural state suitable for

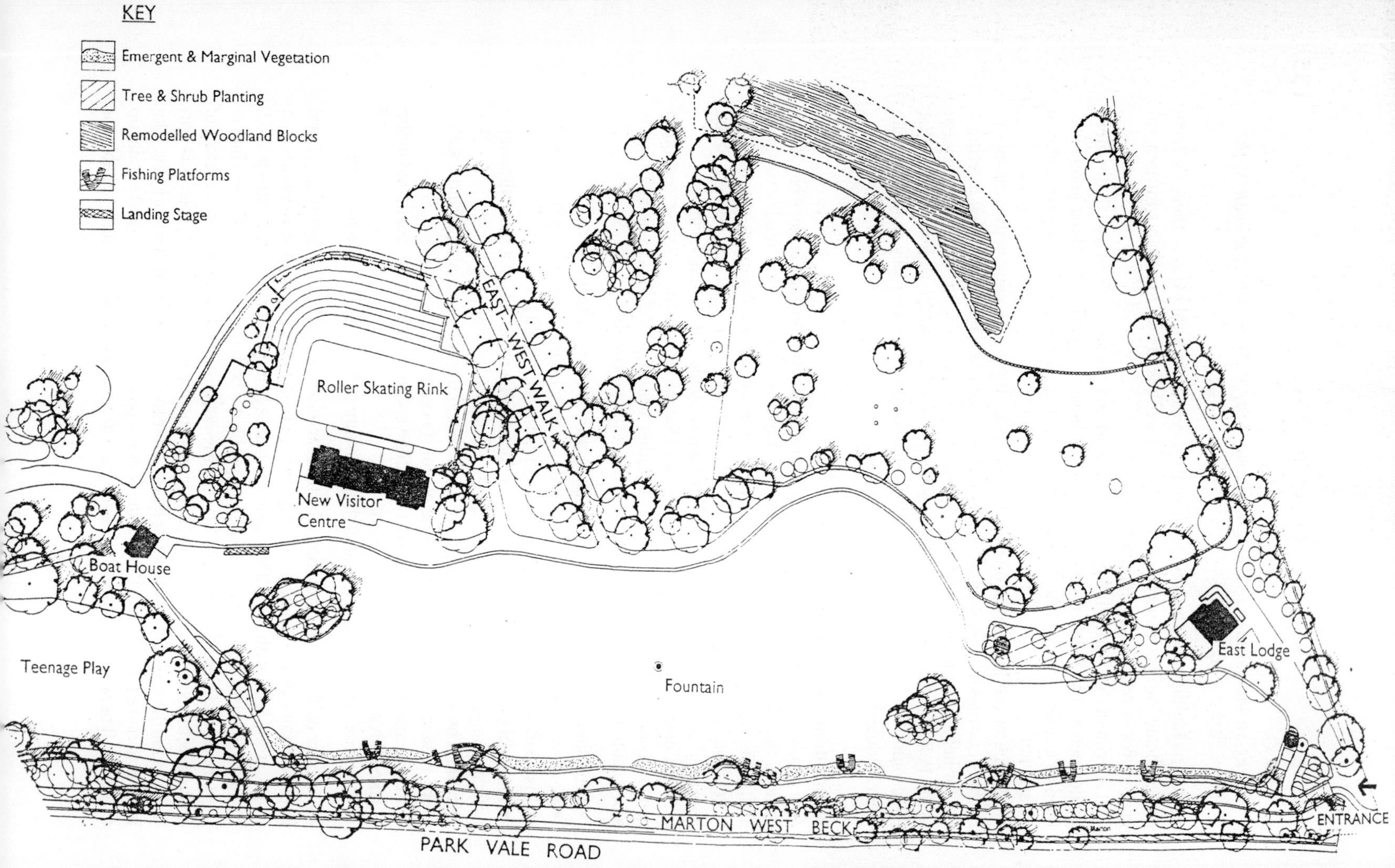

The Master Plan for the re-development of the Lower Lake. Middlesbrough Council Transport and Design Department

KEY

Emergent & Marginal Vegetation
Tree & Shrub Planting
Remodelled Woodland Blocks
Fishing Platforms
Landing Stage

ENTRANCE

East Lodge

Fountain

MARTON WEST BECK

PARK VALE ROAD

EAST — WEST WALK

Roller Skating Rink

New Visitor Centre

Boat House

Teenage Play

Cleaning out the Lower Lake after draining. Photo Tansee Cartwright

habitation by fish, which will not be re-introduced until much later in the year.

The Friends of Albert Park have always taken a particular interest in the restoration and development of the Lower Lake and, thanks to their application in conjunction with Middlesbrough Council, the Northumbrian Water Environmental Trust eventually provided a grant of £73,373 towards the cost of these works. This is a significant proportion of the total cost of £275,600 for this scheme and represents a private sector contribution within the Restoration Programme.

The Former Playground

In close proximity to the paddling pool at the south end of the boating lake was the original playground, of which I myself have many fond memories. Though far less sophisticated than its modern counterpart in Sector 2, it was a place where we could both let off steam and, if we chose, live quite dangerously.

On 20 April 1926, the Park Committee ordered that the Curator should prepare a report on the 'Reservation of Ground in Albert Park for Children' and he presented the following at the meeting of 11 May:

> *As ordered at your last Meeting, I also report on the above matter.*
>
> *The present swing erections which are specially set apart for young children up to 14 years of age, are, I am sorry to say, a great source of trouble to us, particularly the boys' swings at the N.E. corner, which are generally monopolised by a certain type of young man and woman who visit these swings for no good purpose. I am afraid until these portions of ground are fenced in this trouble will continue and I suggest that an amount be included in the Estimates next year to cover such costs.*
>
> *I also recommend that in the near future (providing the Committee can agree*

The original children's playground in 1934, showing the tea-pot lid in the centre.
Middlesbrough Reference Library

with my proposal), a portion of ground should be set aside with certain playground equipment, same to be enclosed and reserved for the small children only, say boys to 10 years and girls to 14 years of age, this being the method adopted in some of the London Parks. Such ground to be laid out in the vicinity of the Paddling Pool, keeping all these playground portions to one end of the Park. We have such a large number of children coming in to use the swings that to erect another set or two would be highly appreciated, and I strongly recommend same myself, as the use of playground equipment keeps children out of mischief.

The Curator had clearly done his homework on the subject and had a sound philosophy about the benefits of keeping children occupied. It is, therefore, surprising that Members did not make any order relating to the implementation of these recommendations. It was, indeed, to be several years before the matter was given further consideration, being raised once again by Samuel Rymer, who had, incidentally, been elevated in the meantime from Park Curator to Parks Superintendent. On 9 December 1930, he inserted the following paragraph into his report to Committee:

CHILDREN'S PLAYGROUND EQUIPMENT

I would also urge the Committee to make more provision at the play centre, near the sand hole and the paddling pool, for in the Albert Park the children are badly catered for in this respect, especially so, when one stops to think that this Park is now some 62 years old and many things are necessary to modernise the Albert Park, that it may be kept in line with your new Grounds, now in the course of lay-out and also with Parks in other boroughs. I suggest an amount be included in the forthcoming Estimates for moving the present swings (the only equipment now provided), down near the paddling pool, and that you also consider the question of purchasing some extra equipment, such as see-saws, joy-wheel, ocean wave, the slide &c., the cost of which might be estimated by Mr. Burgess. I can assure the Committee, this is the finest thing you can do, if you desire to improve the amenities of your Parks.

(It should be noted that the Mr Burgess referred to here was the Borough Engineer and that by this time the Committee had responsibility for two Parks, following the opening in 1928 of Stewart Park, on the southern outskirts of Middlesbrough at Marton).

On this occasion, Members were persuaded that the scheme should go ahead and it was ordered that it should be included in the estimates for the coming financial year. The Superintendent obviously had to hand the precise names of the recommended equipment and I find it interesting to attempt to balance these with my own childhood memories of the playground itself.

There was an array of swings and a slide, together with a long rocking horse, which could accommodate several bums at the same time, but I seem to remember that it was the 'tea-pot lid' which caused the most excitement. I wonder if this could have been the 'joy-wheel'?

In effect, it was a mini-roundabout which was activated by muscle-power. With one foot on the running-board, the other on the ground, and a firm double-handed grip on a push-bar each, we were off, gaining speed as we scooted along. We then sat on top of the spinning structure until dizziness led to the onset of nausea and escape was essential. The trick was to jump off at speed and to hit the ground running. There was always a sneaky feeling that if you got it wrong you might go into orbit. Furthermore, in those days there was no such thing as safety surfaces for the protection of flesh and bone, survival depending upon one's ability to bounce.

Another communal contraption was in the form of a circular bench-seat suspended by metal bars and pivoted on top of a tall pole. There was a rail to lean on while seated and feet were used to push off, with the whole structure circling and swaying precariously. This gave the effect of being on board ship on a stormy sea and could well have been the 'ocean wave'. No matter what they were called, however, the simple fact was that these instruments of pleasurable torture were a source of great delight to us as youngsters.

As we saw earlier, the area of the playground was increased by some 200 square feet in 1955, due to the reduction in the length of the sand pit. At the same time, arrangements were made to move a surplus forty-foot slide and a set of baby swings from Stewart Park for erection at Albert Park, at an estimated cost of £60. On 6 July 1956, the Superintendent was authorised to purchase another piece of playground equipment, described as a 'Junglegym', at a cost of £98, then on 5 July of the following year he was authorised to purchase an outdoor gymnasium set for £60. Just over four years later, on 19 October 1962, the go-ahead was given for the purchase of a Whirling Platform, a ten-foot Merry-go-round and a set of eight-foot high swings with cradle seats, at a total cost of £285 12s.

The Teenage Play Area

As we have seen, one of the main aims of the Restoration Programme is to reinstate earlier features of the Park and it is very interesting to see that this approach has led to proposals for the re-use of the area of the former playground, now designated as a Teenage Play Area for youngsters aged between twelve and sixteen. Public consultation made it clear that such a facility was essential for this age group, also bearing in mind the needs of the less able, and that the refurbished area would act as a focus for youngsters visiting the Park.

Consumer research for this scheme included a workshop session in the Park for 300 pupils from four secondary schools which are situated within walking distance of the Park itself. As a direct result of this get-together, three distinct activity areas have been designed to cater for their requirements, which did not include traditional playground equipment. There is to be an adventure play area, a seating area catering for the need to 'hang out', and a sports area for football, basketball and skateboarding. The Master Plan costing for this scheme was £175,000 and the majority of the installation work was completed by Christmas 2001.

It is seen as important to retain the existing railings of this area, in order to both keep out dogs and to maintain a clearly-defined boundary. It seems safe to assume that these railings date from 1958, when they were introduced as replacements for the originals, which were removed for scrap during the Second World War. Local residents had complained about the late-evening noise from youngsters spilling out from the open area of the original playground and the Committee decided that enclosure was the answer to the problem. Given the planning-stage and on-going involvement of the younger generation in the restoration scheme, they should certainly feel a personal interest in its ultimate success.

SECTOR 3

The Cricket Ground

In the south-east sector of the original Park design, there were two main features: the Cricket Ground and the Exhibition Ground. The former was described as follows at the time of the official opening:

> *Taking the other walk from the lower lake, the cricket ground is reached. It is nearly five acres in extent, and of ample dimensions for playing the game, within a plateau twelve feet wide, and inclined six inches towards the centre, thus giving bystanders a better view of the play than if it had remained level.*

The Park Committee found it difficult to safeguard the playing surface and on 8 May 1873, Members ruled that children should not be allowed to have access to the area. Four years later, however, a more serious matter was under consideration. On 2 July 1879, a letter of complaint was presented in relation to the poor condition of the Ground. The drastic effects of football-playing on the Archery Ground were noted earlier and it was reported at that same meeting, held on 23 December 1879, that this was also true of the Cricket Ground:

> *The football players are now using the Cricket ground, which is also in a very bad state and made worse by the players making holes in the ground to place their goal posts in.*

The writer of the article on the Park in the *Middlesbrough Daily Exchange* of 18 May 1881 made the following observations, clearly expressing his concern over the misuse of the Cricket Ground:

> *The cricket ground will not be in such good condition this year as it has been in*

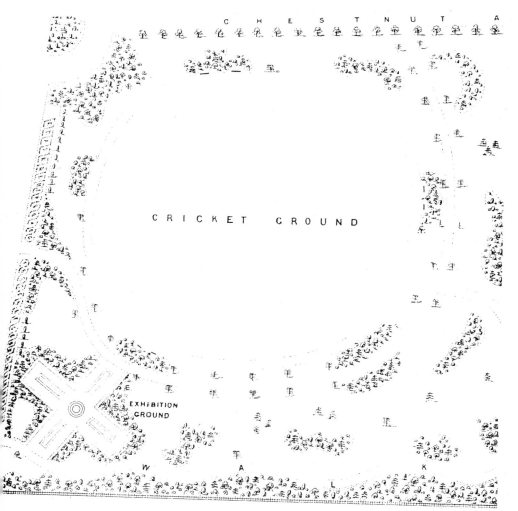

The Cricket Ground and Exhibition Ground, from the 1868 plan of the Park. Teesside
Archives Department

*previous seasons. This portion of the park has now no rest all the year round, for
as soon as the cricketing season comes to an end the football season commences,
and in this way young Middlesbrough will not allow the ground to grow under its
feet. The archery ground is now used for cricket and football. It would be an
excellent plan if one part of the park could be closed to cricket each year, so as to
allow the grass to grow in readiness for the next. If there were two good cricket
grounds in the park this might be done, but under present arrangements it would
seem as if juvenile Middlesbrough would have to be content with the
accommodation as it is.*

By January 1885, great concern was being expressed by the Secretaries of eight
cricket clubs using the Ground and the Curator was instructed to re-turf and roll the
worst-affected areas. At the same time it was decided that footballers should be
barred from the Ground, but that they could continue to use the Archery Ground.

Succeeding Minute references highlight the on-going problem of maintaining the

Cricket Ground and at a meeting held on 11 December 1923 the Curator described it as being in a 'deplorable condition'. He was having trouble in obtaining turf from local sites where the Borough Engineer was involved in excavation works and he also estimated that 200 loads of soil would be needed for levelling the ground, which was six inches lower than it should have been. He was authorised to carry out all necessary works, but this appears to be the last reference to the Cricket Ground as such in the actual Minutes.

In view of its size, the area was subsequently used for the staging of major events and this tradition has been formalised within the recommendations of the Restoration Master Plan. Designated as the Events Area, it is to have improved vehicular access, with improved hardstanding provision for large vehicles actually supporting events. A water supply is to be directed to the site and the important feature of the surrounding tree pattern is to be maintained. The Master Plan costing for this scheme was £99,900.

The Exhibition Ground

There were several original Park features which really caught the attention of the commentator in the *Middlesbrough and Stockton Gazette* of 14 August 1868 and the Exhibition Ground was one of them, being situated in the south-western corner of Sector 3:

Upon the southern side of the walk is the exhibition ground, which is set out upon an original plan, so far as our knowledge extends. It is in the form of a terrace with four wings and a centre rising by tiers to a height of 5 feet 6 inches from the ground. The two outer sides, or tables, are 31 feet long, and 2 feet 6 inches in height; the four wings are each 54 feet long, with two tiers, respectively 2 feet 6 inches and 4 feet high, and a centre in three tiers, 2 feet 6 inches, 4 feet, and 5 feet 6 inches from the ground, with grass walks all round them.

The various tiers of this show ground are built of slag, and then covered with earth, with a growth of grass, thus rendering unnecessary the deal boards generally found as flower stands at horticultural shows. Another advantage of these raised embankments is that five different sizes of tents may be used, according to the requirements of the case. For a small show, the centre would be sufficient, and for larger shows the wings might be taken in as was thought necessary. A still further advantage of the embankments is that two pic-nics can be held upon a small scale, each separated so as to be private from the other, and that treats for school children could be set out upon these natural tables to accommodate two or three thousand at once.

The front and sides of the embankment are now planted with ivy, ferns, moss, polyanthuses, crocuses, primroses, periwinkle, winter aconites, snowdrops, and other dwarf-growing plants that will come in character with the rest. It will thus be seen that this show ground, when not in use, is no common ornament to the park itself. At the outer edge of the ground a number of young trees are planted, which, when grown, will effectually screen the show from the observation of outsiders.

Even though it may have been a novel concept and an impressive structure in its own right, the Exhibition Ground was, unfortunately, to prove to be one of the Park's less enduring features. In this respect, the following extract from the *Middlesbrough Weekly Exchange* of 9 September 1870 is most enlightening:

> *There is one alteration which Mr Cleeton, after considerable perseverance, is likely to succeed in inducing the Park Committee to consent to – the removal of those creations which remind one of Druidical altars, being composed of heaps of stones covered with grass, and which were placed there for the convenience of exhibiting plants in case of a flower show in the Park. As, however, the place is public property, no charge for admission could be made to a flower show there. The holding of one, therefore, is impracticable, and consequently the ugly creations alluded to are neither use nor ornament.*
>
> *Mr Cleeton proposes to substitute an ornamental flower garden on the side of these structures with promenade round it and above it, from which the public can look down upon a gay parterre beneath. As we cannot see the advantage either for picturesqueness or utility of the present hideous concerns which deface that part of the Park, we trust Mr Cleeton's excellent suggestion will be carried out.*

It would appear that the writing was on the wall for the Exhibition Ground from this early stage and, as we saw earlier, the Park Committee Minutes of 6 February 1878 record the fact 'that the sides of the new Lake on the North side of the Park be lined with slag, and that the slag be obtained from the mounds on the South side of the Park'.

An interesting tailpiece on the ill-fated Exhibition Ground is to be found in the *Middlesbrough Daily Exchange* of 6 September 1883:

> *In what was once intended to be the show ground – a series of natural banks for the exhibition of flowering plants – nature has now been allowed to run wild.*

In describing the terrain as 'a series of natural banks', 'A Rambler' is saying, in effect, that it was as though the man-made contours had never existed, and it seems to be a pity that the undertaking had turned out to be such a failure. By the same token, however, it could be argued that a fuller consideration of the scheme at the design stage could have saved a great deal of time and effort. In recent years, the southern perimeter of the site has been allocated for use as a canine toilet and one wonders if Rover and Rex may well have been expressing a personal opinion about the Exhibition Ground concept.

Band Stands

Band music was a very popular feature of activities in the Park from a very early date, the Middlesbrough Police Band probably being the first to be involved in presenting a concert there. Local works' bands and military bands also entertained the crowds of visitors on Summer outings. The original band stand was purchased from George Smith & Co of Glasgow and erected in Sector 3 in the Summer of 1871, to the west of the Cricket Ground. According to the *Middlesbrough Weekly Exchange* of 10 August 1871:

> *A beautiful octagonal iron stand for the band stand is approaching completion and*

The first band stand, erected in 1871. Courtesy Tansee Cartwright

is an ornament to the centre of the Park, the light columns and elegant roof giving the structure quite an oriental aspect.

In 1890 the Park Committee decided that it should be replaced by a new one near the North Lake in Sector 2, the latter's completion being reported on 29 July of that year. The recommended cost was not to exceed £100, but the accepted tender was actually for £112. On 27 January 1891, it was ordered that the old band stand should be converted into a shelter. Even so, it is interesting to note that both structures are referred to as band stands on the Ordnance Survey map of 1894 and, four years later, in a description of the Park by James Paling. This was published in the fascinating little book, by various authors, entitled *Middlesbrough, Its History, Environs and Trade.*

On 14 May 1918, the Borough Engineer was instructed to construct a temporary extension to the band stand, the Committee having received complaints from visiting bands that it was too small.

Concerts were nearly always extremely popular, but for many years, no arrangements had been considered for the provision of chairs for music lovers, who were expected to stand or sit on the grass. This situation was eventually rectified and on 21 April 1925 it was decided that the hire charge on ordinary occasions should be 2d per chair. Committee Members had clearly hoped that this would be a steady source of income, but the Curator reported on 14 July that progress was slower than had been anticipated. He did feel, however, that there would be an improvement once the public became more familiar with the new system. He issued the following returns for eight concerts held between May and July:

Date	Number Seated	Amount Taken		
		£	s	d
31 May	137	1	2	10
1 June	23		3	10
7 June	118		19	8
14 June	465	3	17	6
21 June	101		16	10
28 June	374	3	2	4
5 July	513	5	17	6
12 July	585	4	17	6

There is no indication as to aspirations in terms of the estimated number of bums on seats, but just over 2,300 and an income of over £20 does not seem too bad.

On 8 June 1962, it was reported to Committee that the 'concert platform' had been demolished, being completely beyond repair in view of its dilapidated and extremely dangerous condition. The Chairman turned down a suggestion that a temporary structure should be erected in the skating rink and indicated that a marquee would be made available for concerts planned for that year.

There is still no structural venue in the Park for musical events and it will be a wonderful reinstatement of an early feature when a band stand is re-created slightly north of the original site in Sector 3 as part of the Restoration Project. The new ornamental metal structure will be similar to the original in both style and character and will stand on a brick and stone plinth in keeping with the character of the Park Lodges.

The new band stand will actually be closer to the fountain than its predecessor and is to be separated from the area around the fountain itself by shrubs. These will be designed to act as a back-drop and spatial definition for both the fountain and the band stand. The structure itself will have disabled access and a semi-circular area of hard paving will accommodate audience seating. The position of the band stand on the edge of the extensive Events Area will mean that it can be used for larger functions than normal musical concerts. The Master Plan costing for this scheme was £99,100.

The Roller Skating Rink

On 26 April 1946, members of the Parks Committee considered a letter which was to lead to the creation of a novel feature in Sector 3.

The letter was an enquiry about the possibility of establishing rollerskating in the Park and the matter was given serious consideration. Having decided that a rink should, in fact, be constructed, the site recommended on 11th December 1946 was that facing the Boating Lake, between the main walk and the boathouse. It was reported on 29 May 1947 that the work of excavation had commenced and, on 11 July, that this work was nearly completed. As we will see, the spoil from this exercise was put to good use in another Park project. The rink itself was actually opened on 3 September of the same year and on the 19 September it was reported that it had

The roller skating rink in popular demand in 1957. Middlesbrough Reference Library

already been used by 9,000 adults and children.

A Roller Skating Club had been formed by January 1948 and that year witnessed a rapid increase in the numbers using the rink. On 21 May, it was reported that it had already been used by well over 50,000, while by 24 September the number had further increased to 105,000 and the Superintendent reported that 20,000 had hired the Park skates. The Skating Club had been involved in staging galas and the rink became a venue for championship competitions.

After two years of use, the rink needed to be re-surfaced and its maintenance

Barbara Munroe and her roller skating coach in about 1950. Photo Barbara Harrison

became an on-going problem. From 1950, occasional use was made of the services of a professional skater for instruction classes and on 7 June 1951 it was reported that a total of 9,279 spectators had attended the Whit Holiday galas.

In 1953, consideration was given to the improvement of the area surrounding the rink enclosure and work was undertaken on the erection of public conveniences. Arrangements for lighting the rink were made in the following year, while from the later 1950's consideration was given to the improvement of facilities in terms of the buildings at the rink. This involved the construction of a control room and catering facilities.

Maintenance and re-surfacing have been an on-going problem and Ken Sherwood recorded that on 28 November 1972 the Manchester-based firm which had originally installed the rink began work on re-laying all the terracotta tiles. The rink, once again, fell into a state of disrepair and it has actually been disused for some time.

Under these circumstances, and in line with strong public pressure, plans have been formulated for major improvement works on site as part of the Restoration Plan. There has been a clear demand for the reconstruction of the rink as a venue for strenuous exercise for the younger generation, while the Middlesbrough Roller Hockey Club is also keen to have access to match and training facilities which are in keeping with the minimum standards of the Governing Body for Roller Hockey.

Advice was taken from the City Council in Manchester, where a roller skating rink of such a standard had recently been constructed and the Albert Park rink has been designed to take account of the new Visitor Centre, replacing the original buildings on the site. The load-bearing capability of the surface of the new rink, which was completed in December 2001, will ensure that it can also be used for staging and scaffolding in relation to theatrical and musical events. A significant design element is that of access to the lower tier of the terraced seating for wheelchairs, while pedestrian circulation around the rink is to be widened. The Master Plan costing for this scheme was £228,100.

The late-1950's amenities block at the roller skating rink, demolished in 2001. Photo Tansee Cartwright

The newly-completed Visitor Centre in January 2002, occupying the site of the roller skating rink amenities block. Photo George Ward

The New Visitor Centre

At the time of the Restoration survey, the roller skating rink buildings were found to be both unattractive and in a structurally poor condition. Facilities included changing rooms, toilets and a tea room, all of which clearly needed to be replaced. With the re-development of the site, the opportunity has been taken to provide a building which will fulfil a much wider range of functions, being both contemporary in design while, at the same time, in character with the original Victorian buildings in the Park.

The building faces both the skating rink and the lake, with glazed elevations which allow views through the central circulation area from one side of the building to the

The newly-resurfaced roller skating rink and the west front of the Visitor Centre in January 2002. Photo George Ward

other. Most visitors are expected to approach from the lakeside footpath, named on the original plan of the Park as the East Walk, and for that reason the main entrance and reception area are on that side of the building, together with the public toilets.

All the needs of the skaters are catered for and there is also a high quality tea room. A self-contained area for community and creche use is provided, with its own toilet facilities. Public opinion was strongly in favour of the appointment of a Park Ranger or Manager, who is to be based in the new Centre, the completion of which was scheduled for January 2002. The general administration and oversight of the Park will be co-ordinated here, in conjunction with the staff who work in the Pavilion. The Master Plan costing for this scheme was £412,400.

<u>SECTOR 4</u>

In the original design, the focal point of Sector 4 was the Upper Lake, associated with which were two artefacts, both of considerable historical interest, but from widely diverse eras: the Crimean Cannon and the Norman Arch.

The Upper Lake or Cannon Lake

The earliest description of the Upper Lake appeared in the *Middlesbrough and Stockton Gazette* of 14 August 1868:

> *Following the path to the south boundary for a short distance, we turn up the 'Lover's Walk', and passing through a rustic archway, come suddenly and unexpectedly upon an ornamental lake, surrounded by a footpath, bordered with rockwork, and passing under three rustic arches. From what we hear this is thought most highly of as being a 'bit of fairy land', almost every visitor to the park going there first... The embankments round the lake are planted with tall trees, creepers, small shrubs, climbers, &c. Specimens of the variegated Japan honeysuckle (which is generally treated as a greenhouse plant) have been growing upon the embankment here for above two years, and are doing remarkably well. Immediately facing the ancient arch before mentioned a seat is placed, so as to command a view of the water, rockwork, rustic arches, and shrubs upon the opposite side, forming a scene for a picture such as we rarely meet with. In the centre of the lake there is an island that would be a suitable resort for aquatic fowls, and these will complete the appearance of this, the most effective bit of scenery to be found in the park, and, it will be admitted, an honour to the designer and executor.*

We saw earlier that the supply of water to the Lower Lake was a cause of concern for the Park Committee, and there is an interesting insight into this aspect of the Upper Lake in the *Middlesbrough Daily Exchange* of 18 May 1881:

> *At the time of our visit the lake was rather muddy, and upon enquiry as to the cause, we were told that the supply of water was derived from the surface drainage. A great improvement could be made in this lake by widening it at the lower end which now has a stelly appearance, and looks altogether too circumscribed.*

The word 'stell' was used locally to denote a natural watercourse, such as a stream or a beck.

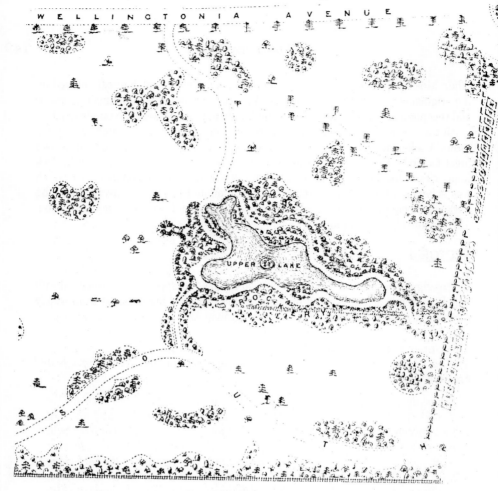

The Upper Lake, or Cannon Lake, from the Park plan of 1868. Teesside Archives Department

On 26 March 1889, the Curator reported to the Park Committee on the problem of a leakage in the lake, apparently caused by an old drain. While attempting to drain the lake prior to cleaning it in 1925, it was discovered that the drain itself was actually blocked and the subsequent build-up of water led to a serious situation in relation to the boiler used for heating the greenhouses. During the drama which ensued, the Curator found himself flying by the seat of his pants, as we may see from his detailed report to Committee on 17th November 1925:

CANNON LAKE – DRAIN STOPPAGE
On Monday the 2nd inst., the Borough Engineer commenced to drain the water from the above lake, preparatory to the cleaning out of same. For several days after the valve was opened at the lake this drain was running very satisfactorily, but on the Saturday morning it was evident it had become partly stopped up, for the man in charge of this work was having some trouble with same. All gulleys at the Greenhouses, Stokehold, etc., are connected into this drain, making it essentially necessary that this should be kept clear. Consequently, I pointed out to the man the seriousness of this matter, but he assured me that having practically shut off the

lake there was no danger of a complete stoppage. He left the Park about 11.00 a.m. and at 12 o'clock it was apparent that the water was rising in the gulleys at the greenhouse, so I ordered one of my own men to fasten up the valve at the lake altogether in the hope that this would prove effective, but we had exceptionally heavy rainfall that day, and water coming from the land was finding its way into the drain also making things worse than ever.

At 2.30 p.m. my Foreman returned to his boilers and the water had risen some six to eight inches in the stokehold; he attempted to bale out, but after two hours work the water was higher than when he commenced, and despite his efforts, the boiler fire was extinguished about 5 p.m. Fortunately it was not very cold, and having good pipe heat in the Greenhouses, this carried us through the night, but on the Sunday morning a bitter wind was blowing, every appearance of snowfall and perhaps keen frost throughout the Sunday night, which would have proved fatal to many pounds worth of valuable plants in the Greenhouses.

As the Committee will understand, the situation was now very serious and it was imperative that we should have the boiler fire with as little delay as possible. We had now about two and a half feet of water around the boiler, but having no rain through the Saturday night, I thought it might be possible to get rid of most of the water by baling and attempted to do so. However, there must have been thousands of gallons of water, for after two hours baling we had made no impression and it was quite clear to me that it was absolutely futile to try and clear this by hand. I therefore considered it my duty to requisition the Trailer Pump from the Fire Brigade Department and went to the Fire Superintendent to arrange for same. Whilst there I tried to get into communication with the Borough Engineer, but he was not at home then, so I rang up the town clerk and informed him of my intentions, explaining the situation to him and he agreed I was doing the right thing.

I am glad to say that after an hour's pumping operation we were clear and had the boiler fire going again. Unfortunately, this turned out to be only a temporary relief, for I visited the Greenhouses about half past six at night and again we had from six to seven inches of water in the Stokehold, and rising every minute, within two hours the fire would be out again. I again telephoned the Borough Engineer and explained what had been done and how serious this matter was, and as the Thermometer was now registering 6 degrees of frost, the fire must be kept going at all costs, even should they continue pumping throughout the night. He agreed that if necessary this must be done and it was found to be so, one of my own men, along with the Fire Superintendent's man staying the night through and pumping water every two hours, until 7 a.m. Monday morning. We kept it cleared throughout the day by baling from the chambers, and all was well until 11 p.m. they had again to pump for about two hours, after which I am pleased to say no more pumping was required.

The Borough Engineer had by now got a passage through the drain which kept us clear and everything was out of danger. I am glad to say that the drain is now running normally and the Borough Engineer is having additional inspection chambers fixed to avoid similar occurrences in the future.

Having made sure that his current problems were solved, it is just as well that the

Curator was not able to see too far into the future, for by 1947 it was decided that the Cannon Lake should actually be filled in. The Borough Engineer presented the following report to the Parks Committee on 21 March of that year:

CANNON LAKE – ALBERT PARK. – As instructed, I have prepared a scheme and estimate for the filling-in of this lake.

In order to drain the area effectively, it will be necessary to lay a new 6 inch drain to pick up the existing drains discharging into the lake, which will connect to the existing drain running eastwards towards the lower lake. A land drain will also be laid in the bed of the lake before filling-in.

The filling for the lake will be obtained from the mounds lying round the lake, or alternatively, if this scheme is carried out concurrently with the skating rink, about half the necessary filling can be obtained from the surplus excavating of the latter job. In either case, the cost will be about the same.

A new path will be made near the western side of the lake, to connect with the existing path near the cannon, and the path running parallel with Park Road South.

The total cost is estimated at £1,200, excluding any turfing and planting.

In the event, spoil from the excavation of the roller skating rink was utilised for the in-fill and three months later, on 20 June 1947, it was reported that it was completed, a fact which marked the disappearance of another of the Park's major original features. On 8 November 1949, it was reported that the fencing which had surrounded the lake had been removed from the site, thus releasing a two-acre area for public access.

Redevelopment plans for the Park which were evolved in 1984 led to the creation of new water features, consisting of small lakes, falls and bridges, to the west of the site of the old Cannon Lake. The work for this scheme was contracted out in August 1986 for the sum of £76,652. Interest in the site came to the fore once again in the Stage One Restoration Plan of July 1998, when it was proposed that the original lake should be reinstated, together with associated planting and the two historical features to be considered below.

At that early stage in the proceedings, the proposal received the enthusiastic backing of English Heritage, but on the occasion of their site visit in April 2000, accompanied by a representative of the Heritage Lottery Fund, the consensus of opinion was that it would be advisable to withdraw the proposal from the Stage Two submission. This sentiment reinforced the reservations then entertained by Middlesbrough Council itself, after further consideration by its own consultation team, and the Cannon Lake proposal was duly withdrawn, apart from minor alterations to the lay-out of footpaths in the area to the west of the former Depot site. The Master Plan costing for this scheme was £20,000.

In some respects, both historical and aesthetic, it is regrettable that the original proposal to reinstate the lake was not put into effect. It is, however, interesting to note that the area of the 1984 water features is to be landscaped in order to enhance their overall setting, the decision having been made not to replace the existing bridges. The Master Plan costing for this scheme was £18,000.

The Crimean Cannon

This Russian artillery-piece was a relic of the siege of Sebastopol, in the Crimean War, which began in September 1854 and lasted for a year. The victors found themselves in possession of many such cannon as trophies of war and Lord Panmure, the Secretary for War, made them available to local authorities in England.

Middlesbrough Borough Council submitted an application for a cannon in 1857 and one was earmarked for delivery in the following year. Ideas were then considered for the best place to place the cannon from the point of view of public access and public safety. Interestingly enough, the Council felt that the ideal setting for its display would have been in a public park, but in the absence of such an amenity it was to occupy a number of sites.

It spent some time in the gas works yard, then suggestions to mount it either near the Corporation boat landing or in the Market Place were turned down. A site near St Hilda's Parish Church, in the north-east corner of Market Place itself, was used for some time, then with the commencement of the work of laying-out Albert Park in 1866, the cannon was transferred to that location. It was, in fact, actually fired as part of the celebrations associated with the first tree-planting in February of that year. A plinth was created for its display and it was mounted at the Upper Lake, to which it subsequently gave its more familiar name.

In 1948, subsequent to the filling-in of the Cannon Lake, the gun itself became part of the collections of the Middlesbrough Museums Service and it was moved to Stewart Park, where it remained until May 1965. Ken Sherwood remembers that it was kept there in a wood and that it proved to be of some interest to rabbits. On one

The Crimean Cannon on its lakeside plinth. Middlesbrough Reference Library

The Crimean Cannon and ancient boulder at the Dorman Museum. Photo George War

The Cannon Lake, showing the Crimean Cannon in relation to the Norman Arch. Author's collection

occasion, their tracks in the snow led to the barrel of the gun, from which the intruders were flushed out and caught.

Having narrowly escaped being broken up for scrap, the cannon was transferred from Stewart Park to the Territorial Army base on Stockton Road. It remained there until 1978, when it was moved once again, to take up a position outside the Dorman Museum, where it was in the company of the ancient boulder which formerly stood inside the Park gates. The Museum authorities were later informed by a specialist researcher that the cannon is a 25-pounder, firing a 6-inch ball, and that its inscriptions indicate that it was cast in 1824.

Twenty years later, it was earmarked for a further move, this time back into the Park, as a feature of the reinstated Cannon Lake, but that, as we have seen, was a proposed project which did not actually come to fruition. There was still, however, a strong feeling that the cannon itself should, in fact, be returned to the Park and the opportunity arose for it to be incorporated into the Albert Park Memorial Garden project, the results of which we admired in Sector 1 when our walkabout began.

This latest, and hopefully final, move was made on Friday, 30 November 2001 and I was very pleased to be an eye witness to this small piece of history-in-the-making. The actual move was undertaken by J Hewitt Crane Hire Ltd of the Tees Offshore Base at South Bank and there was a heart-stopping moment at lift-off, when the cannon swung towards the Museum wall and had to be pulled away manually in mid-air. I was particularly keen to know the weight of the cannon and was told that it had registered on the crane's control panel as 3.2 tons.

It was a most unusual sight as it was swung easily on to the back of a lorry, by which it was transferred into the Park through the main gates. The crane then had to follow, with a careful manoeuvre through the gates, and the cannon was soon airborne once again, this time en route for its resting-place at the east end of the Memorial Garden. The actual base used had come to light during the course of the groundwork for the Memorial Garden and was identified as the support for Henry Bolckow's statue, which had been placed on that site in 1925. Touch-down for the cannon was at 2.40 p.m. and it was immediately acknowledged by on-lookers as being an ideal addition to the Memorial Garden. After being away for over half a century, it was back home in the Park, where it is bound to be an early attraction for all visitors.

The Norman Arch

From the very outset of its creation, Albert Park was of great interest to local residents and there is evidence to show that one of them may well have been instrumental in inspiring the construction of one its more unusual landmarks.

In the *Middlesbrough Weekly News and Cleveland Advertiser* of 27 July 1866, the designer William Barratt became the focus of attention for the writer of the *Local Gossip* column, who was clearly taking a close personal interest in the progress of laying-out the Park. His remarks are significant in drawing attention to the heritage of Middlesbrough's pre-industrial past and the way in which he felt that the Park should play a part in both preserving and demonstrating that heritage:

> *I have a hint for Mr Barratt, the designer and layer out of our new park. The other*

Park visitors at the Norman Arch. Ken Sherwood Collection

day in passing along one of our suburban thoroughfares I almost stumbled over a large stone, which on close inspection I found to be a portion of the ancient remains of the priory which existed in Middlesbrough in the days of yore. The stone was evidently a portion of the semicircular arch of a Norman window, there being a round moulding on the angle, and above that the characteristic chevron ornament.

I am informed that a number of these stones, relics of the hoary past, the Middlesbro' of ancient days, are to be had at Newport, whither they were carried from Middlesbrough at the time when it was proposed to build a church there out of the ruins of the priory of St Hilda. Could not Mr Barratt by some means get possession of these old stones and place them in a suitable position in the park, where they would serve to tell a story of our past history?

I think a few stones of the old priory are not unfit mementoes to be placed in the park, and moreover it is a pity that such relics of hoar antiquity should be put to the base uses which they now serve. I hope Mr Barratt will take the matter up.

The matter was, indeed, taken up and these stones were formed into one of the most interesting features of the Park, as described in the *Middlesbrough and Stockton Gazette* of 14 August 1868:

Upon the north side of the (Upper) lake, we find an ancient-looking stone arch *erected, in which some remains of the ancient church at Newport are introduced; as also suitable contributions by several local gentlemen. It is intended that this and the other arches shall be overgrown with ivy and various creepers.*

It seems reasonable to assume that the arch, as a structure, did not represent an actual architectural feature of the Middlesbrough Priory, which, incidentally, occupied a site in the modern North Street, in the St Hilda's area of Old Middlesbrough. It was, most likely, a symbolic creation from available remains of the monastery.

The arch itself proved to be a very popular feature at the Cannon Lake and stood as what appeared to be a solid reminder of Middlesbrough's ancient past. The Park Committee Minutes, however, reveal that it did, in fact, require repairing on several occasions from as early as 1876. Within two years, on 8 May 1878, the surveyor was instructed to repair the structure in order to make it secure, while in 1899 actual reconstruction was necessary, after it had been blown down.

In 1911, the Park Committee received a request to sanction virtual vandalism of the arch, in the form of a letter from the Rev. Frank Harrison Stock, Vicar of St Hilda's Parish Church. He asked for their agreement to the removal of four Norman stones from the arch, so that they might be made available for preservation within his church. Mr Stock's request was considered and sanctioned on 18 July, but that was not the end of the matter.

A similar request was received in 1915, relating to other stones in the pillars of the arch, and the Committee agreed on 21 December that they, too, could be handed over. However, this decision was rescinded on 18 January 1916, after it had been

In addition to the elegant stonework of the Norman Arch, the park was also adorned with several rustic arches, one of which is shown here soon after the opening in 1868.
Teesside Archives Department

queried by the Town Council itself. As though it had suddenly recognised the importance of the arch, the Park Committee ordered that a metal plate should be fixed to it, giving details of its significance.

The structure continued intact until the Cannon Lake was filled in, when it was decided that it should be removed. After demolition, the ancient stones were handed over to the Libraries and Museum Committee for preservation at the Dorman Museum. Following the demolition of St Hilda's Church in 1969, the stones acquired by Vicar Stock were also transferred to the Museum.

Only a small number of the stones were used for display within the Museum, the majority being piled up beyond the south wall of the modern extension to the original building. The stones had to be moved once again in order to make way for a further recent building programme and it was found necessary to actually excavate the lower ones, which had sunk well into the ground because of the overall weight of the pile. They were subsequently moved back into the Park, with a view to recreating the original arch feature at the reinstated Cannon Lake, but, as we have seen, that scheme was abandoned.

Greenhouses and Floral Bedding Displays

As we saw earlier, it was stated at the time of his retirement in 1888 that Edward Cleaton did not have access to a greenhouse when he undertook the laying-out of the

The greenhouses in relation to the Upper Lake, from an undated plan. Author's collection

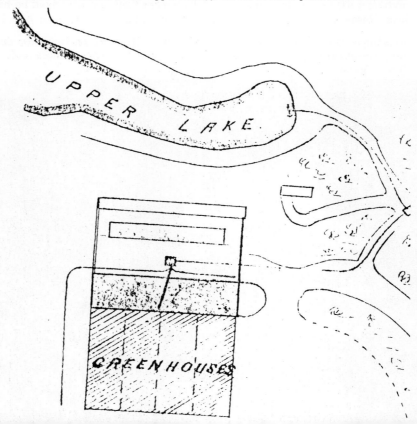

Park in 1866, which must have made an onerous task even more difficult. It must, indeed, have been a great step forward when Propagating Houses were established in the south-east corner of Sector 4.

The earliest reference to 'Glass Houses' which I have found in Committee Minutes appears on 3 February 1870, when the Surveyor was reported as having produced designs and estimates prior to tendering. On 20 March 1871 it also reveals that work was in hand on 'Park Greenhouses' and that the contractor, Mr Fidler, was at fault for not clearing substandard materials from the site. A brief note on 9 October 1873 states that the Glass Houses were completed. It would seem strange if these were the same structures for which designs were drawn up in 1870, unless the whole project had been beset with problems.

Writing in the *Middlesbrough Daily Exchange* of 6 September 1883, 'A Rambler' described these facilities in the following way:

> *At this point I may say that I had an opportunity of inspecting the propagating houses, which occupy a somewhat secluded position to the east of the duck-pond. Last winter a new house was erected 54 ft. long, within which can be accommodated 7,000 plants. The other two houses are 42 ft. in length, and all three are heated with hot water pipes springing from an ordinary saddle-back boiler. The process of propagation from slips for next year was in full swing at the time of my visit, and when I state that there are 35,000 bedding plants – of which 20,000 are geraniums – planted out in the park every year, in addition to annuals and hardy herbaceous plants, it will be seen that the accommodation for propagation and preservation during the winter must be extensive.*

This important facility in the working life of the Park is simply indicated on the 1875 plan of the Park as *Hot House*, then on a series of Ordnance Survey maps from 1894 as *Nursery*. It must have been a hive of activity from the outset – the nerve-centre for

The Park Depot, on the site of the greenhouses. Photo George Ward

maintaining the high standard of floral bedding displays. The area evolved into the Park Depot and it has now been earmarked for development as disabled car parking, with a new gate for vehicular access. The Master Plan costing for this scheme was £16,500. It is intended to retain some of the buildings for continued use in the maintenance of the Park.

Succeeding Curators and Superintendents took great pride in the displays of flowers and plants throughout the Park, some of which are highlighted in the descriptions which appear in my Appendices. The following listing represents a summary of specimens which were of particular interest to the writers of these newspaper articles between 1868 and 1883, also including trees and shrubs:

Acacia	Gorse	Periwinkle
Acuba Japonica	Gum Tree	Petunia
Ageratum	Hawthorn Bushes	Pine, Australian
Ash	Holly	Plane, Oriental
Aspen	Honeysuckle, Japan	Polyanthus
Aucauria	Horse Chestnut	Poplar
Beech, Purple	Hyacinth	Poplar, Italian
Blackberry	Hygeratum	Poplar, Lombardy
Castor Oil Plant	Indian Shot	Primrose
Cedar of Lebanon	Ivy	Rhododendron
Cineraria	Jessamine	Rose
Cirastia	Laurel, Portugal	Rose, Wild
Clematis	Lilac	Snapdragon
Cockspur Grass	Lobelia	Snowdrop
Crocus	Maidenhair Tree	Snow in Summer
Cupressus Lawsoniana	Maritinum White	Sycamore
Dahlia	May	Tregertis
Dark Heath Plant	Moss	Tregetas
Elm	Nasturtium	Tulip
Evergreens	Narcissus	Verbena
Ferns	Oak	Walnut
Flowering Cherry	Oak, Turkey	Wellingtonia
Funkies	Parsley, American	Willow
Geranium	Perella Nancunensis	Winter Aconites

Park Committee Minutes provide information relating to the detailed planning of the floral beds in terms of the Curator's recommendations with regard to the purchase of stock. Those for 22 September 1896, for example, show that he wished to order a total of 9,500 tulip bulbs, consisting of 1,000 each of Duc Von Thol Red and Yellow, Rose, Yellow, Scarlet, White; Keizerskroon, La Reine and Tournesol; and 1,500 of Yellow Prince. He also required 2,000 Narcissus Princeps and 250 each of Blue, White and Red 'Hyacinths'. The Curator had written for prices to eight different firms and these ranged from £28 10s 3d to £19. Over half a century later, on 6 June 1952, it was agreed that 62,650 Dutch bulbs could be purchased for £679 5s. 0d. By that time, of course, the planting at Albert Park formed only part of a much wider area of activity.

The Clock

On our leisurely walk round the Park, we have heard the musical hourly striking of the tower clock at least twice and, as we pause to inspect it now, it is interesting to consider the background to its being there.

The Park Clock, with the West Lodge in the background. Photo Tansee Cartwright

The following letter was read to members of the Park Committee at their meeting of 27 September 1898:

Saltburn, 12 September 1898

To the Chairman of the Park Committee.

Dear Sir, – In looking at the Report of the Park Committee's Meeting, I see where one or two members have said that a Clock would be a great acquisition to the Park. I have consulted a Clockmaker, from the estimate he gave me as to price, &c, for a Clock with two dials 3-feet diameter. I write to say that as my connection with the Corporation will soon terminate, I wish to leave some small memento of my long connection with the Council.

I am, therefore, willing in the event of the Park Committee, or any person or persons, erecting some structure on which the Clock could be fixed, to present a Clock, made and guaranteed by a local Clockmaker.

Hoping this will meet with your approval.

I am, yours truly,

THOMAS SANDERSON.

This generous offer was gratefully accepted by the Park Committee and the ensuing Minutes reveal that the site for the erection of such a clock was a matter of some interest. Alderman Sanderson himself suggested that a clock mechanism might be fixed to the top of the main entrance gate, but on 25 July 1899 the Borough Surveyor advised against this, as the clock itself would be at risk because of the wind and it would be difficult to maintain accurate time.

On 26 September 1899, a year after making his offer of a clock, Thomas Sanderson's suggestion of an alternative design was accepted. He had heard about, and actually visited, a Tower Clock at Douglas, Isle of Man, to the design of W Macfarlane & Co of Glasgow, and offered to provide such a structure for the Park. This proposal was approved and on 27 March 1900 the Surveyor was ordered to proceed with the erection of the clock on the agreed site on the south side of the main walk inside the entrance. On 22 May, it was agreed that the following inscription should be affixed to the cast iron tower of the clock:

This Clock, with the Tower, was presented to the Inhabitants of the Town
by Thomas Sanderson, Esq. JP,
as a memento of his long connection with the Council (as Councillor,
Alderman and Mayor), and with the Borough of Middlesbrough. May, 1900.

The clock was formally started by Mr Sanderson on 28 August 1900 and subsequently, on 25 March 1902 his offer of paying for the installation of a striking mechanism was accepted by Committee. On the occasion of an inspection of the Park on 3 September 1903, the Mayor, Councillor Hedley, activated the striking mechanism.

A century after their creation and installation, the clock and its tower present themselves as perhaps the most challenging of all the historic features of the Park to be conserved during the Restoration Project. The clock is the only mechanism and the tower is by far the tallest structure.

The initial Hirst Conservation Survey of May 2000 revealed that the cast iron tower is in a poor condition, inspection from the ladder revealing corrosion to the joints, and it is clear that once scaffolding is in position even more detailed work will have to be carried out, possibly with the assistance of a structural engineer for expert opinion. Before any programme of conservation works can be undertaken, the actual clock mechanism will have to be removed and it, too, will need to be assessed by an expert in the field.

The tower is supported by a course of red bricks, of inadequate quality and projecting beyond its octagonal base, and they, too, are showing signs of decay. There is rather difficult access to the interior of the base by means of a hatch, which revealed an in-fill of concrete and a small heater, which was presumably installed to counteract condensation.

It was clear to the surveyors that access to the exterior of the base had been much easier for members of the local canine clan, which seem to have regarded the ornately elegant tower as the ultimate Lamp Post from Heaven.

The West Lodge
As was noted earlier, it is the East Lodge which is the more impressive of the two residential buildings within the boundaries of the Park, and it was the West Lodge which was home to the Curators. Erected in 1866, it was designed by Charles J Adams of Stockton.

The West Lodge, erected in 1866 as the Curator's residence. Photo Tansee Cartwright

Adams had also been responsible for designing the magnificent Royal Exchange Buildings, close to Middlesbrough Railway Station, the foundation stone of which was laid by Henry Bolckow on 24 November 1866. On that occasion, a time capsule was inserted with the stone, the objects enclosed including a photograph of the architect himself. During the course of the demolition of the Royal Exchange in February 1985, the time capsule itself was not found, but in the rubble were newspapers, the original estimate for the building and Adams' photograph.

The West Lodge was given Grade II status in the Department of the Environment *List of Buildings of Special Architectural or Historical Interest* (1988), in which document it is described, rather technically, thus:

Red brick, with blue brick and sandstone dressings. Welsh and Lakeland slate roofs with pierced iron ridge crestings and finials. Asymetrical; incorporating Gothic and classical detailing. 1¹/₂ storeys, 2 bays. Double-chamfered plinths. 3 steps up to right 4-panel door in segment-headed hollow-chamfered surround under plaque with arms of Middlesbrough Corporation. Below eaves, moulded brick corbelled frieze, continued on returns. Projected left gabled cross wing had stone one-storey canted bay window whose octagonal pilasters, with individually-carved foliate capitals, frame trefoil-headed sashes under chamfered round heads. Angle water shoots on foliate brackets, below bracketed battered parapet with wrought iron crestings. Battered sills. Pair of segment-headed first-floor sash windows, in hollow-chamfered surrounds, under plaque with arms of H.W.F. Bolckow, in gable. Chamfered gable coping and gabled kneelers. Steeply-pitched hipped and gabled roofs with bands of shaped slates and embattled transverse ridge stacks. Gabled wall monument in screen wall adjoining right; bronze tablet records: 'THIS PARK WAS PRESENTED TO THE PEOPLE OF MIDDLESBROUGH BY HENRY WILLIAM FERDINAND BOLCKOW. OPENED BY PRINCE ARTHUR IN 1868...'; erected 1901. Gable red sandstone monument, right of screen wall, carries original worn (1868) dedication of Park on reverse side. Front has niche, under carved foliate band, to house bust of Bolckow, with brass plate below, both now missing; bust now in Dorman Memorial Museum. 2-bay left return with similar windows. INTERIOR: Open-well staircase with turned balusters and chamfered square newels. Panelled doors in moulded surrounds. Disused and dilapidated at time of survey. Mid C20 one-storey north-west extension not of special interest. Included for historical associations.

A number of points relating to Henry Bolckow and associated memorials will be considered in Chapter Six.

A telling statement relating to the West Lodge is to be found in The *Middlesbrough Weekly Exchange* of 10 August 1871, in the context of the erection of the East Lodge:

A new lodge is being erected at the eastern gate which, we trust, will be more commodious than the one at the western end of the Park which seems to have been erected wholly on the show principle, and is altogether unsuitable as a dwelling.

The Lodge continued in its original state until 1891, when gas was installed, then in

Charles J Adams, the architect who designed the West Lodge, photographed in 1866. Author's Collection

March 1893 the Curator was successful in his bid to have the building extended for the convenience of his family. With the appointment of Harry Courtenay Hildyard as Parks Superintendent in 1943, it was decided that the Lodge was too small to continue in use as a residence and a house at 40 Croydon Road was purchased as its replacement. From that time, the old building became an office and store.

By 1955, it was considered to be too small even for that purpose and after staff were transferred to premises at 304 Linthorpe Road it was re-converted for use as living accommodation.

In 1982, the lodge was under threat of demolition, a fact which led to considerable local opposition. Those involved in calling for its retention included Mr Harry Rymer, then aged eighty-two, of Linthorpe. His father, Henry Rymer, had first come to the Park as foreman in 1886, at the age of twenty-one, and became curator in 1895. Harry himself was born in the old Lodge and had many happy memories of his childhood there.

As a result of the public outcry, the building survived and it was subsequently used as a base for *Take Five*, a group which organised activities for young people. As we saw earlier, it is now used by The Friends of Albert Park and offers facilities as a cafe.

A survey of the West Lodge was carried out by Middlesbrough Council Asset Management personnel and their report of January 2000 indicates that it is in generally good condition. It was, however, decided that minor repairs and external decorating would be required within the next two years.

Thermometer, Barometer and Rain Gauge
Weather conditions have always been significant within the context of the use of the Park and, at quite an early stage, they also proved to be of scientific interest. On 5 January 1871, it was recommended to the Park Committee that a thermometer, barometer and rain gauge should be acquired, and that a register of each should then be kept. At the following meeting, held on 9 February, it was ordered that the instruments were to be obtained from a Mr Thirkell at a cost not exceeding £8. It was stipulated that the barometer was to be of the type used by the Royal Lifeboat Institution.

After the instruments were acquired, meteorological reports were reproduced in the Park Committee Minutes. On 26 August 1887, it was ordered that the thermometer stand should be removed and replaced by a flower bed. As time passed, all of the instruments were moved to the West Lodge and have since been disposed of.

Chapter Five

Public Events and Wartime Activities in the Park

Public Events in the Park

By virtue of its pleasant surroundings and its capacity for large crowds, the Park has always been regarded as an ideal natural venue for the staging of special public events and celebrations. The earliest evidence of a request for an organised gathering appears in the Park Committee Minutes of 21 August 1874, to which members agreed:

The Town Clerk reported that the School Board requested to supply refreshments & to make tea for their School Children in the Park at a treat which they wished to give there on Friday the 28th inst. & they also requested leave to have the Police & probably another band in the Park on the occasion.

Middlesbrough celebrated its Golden Jubilee on 6 October 1881 and there was a fireworks display and tree-planting ceremony in the Park. At the time, it was suggested by William Fallows, the instigator of the celebrations, that the event should be marked with the erection in the Park of a statue in honour of Henry Bolckow, together with a white obelisk. Unfortunately, however, his proposal was not put into effect. It is worthy of note in passing that William Fallows was one of the inaugural tree-planters in the Park in February 1866.

Before the end of the century, two Royal events and a Royal visit were marked with events in the Park. The first of these was Queen Victoria's Golden Jubilee in 1887. On 21 June, some rather low-key celebrations were held in Middlesbrough, the main event being a procession of schoolchildren. This began in the Market Place and ended in the Park, where the youngsters became involved in organised fun and games. Exactly ten years later, events were organised to mark the Queen's Diamond Jubilee.

On 23 January 1889, Middlesbrough's new Municipal Buildings were officially opened by His Royal Highness the Prince of Wales, later to become King Edward VII. On that occasion, a Royal Salute was fired in the Park and the Committee Minutes of 28 January record the interesting fact that this caused damage to the Refreshment Rooms, breaking three windows and dislodging tiles from the roof.

September 13 1905 witnessed a Garden Party and Fete by courtesy of Sir Samuel and Lady Sadler, the estimated attendance being 'over 100,000', and the Coronation of King George V and Queen Mary was celebrated in June 1911. It is recorded that an extra twelve men had to be drafted in to clear up after the latter event. In October of the same year, His Royal Highness the Duke of Connaught, whose father had actually opened the Park forty-three years earlier, opened Middlesbrough's highly-regarded Transporter Bridge and the Kirby Secondary School, at Linthorpe. He marked his visit by planting a tree in the Park.

Under normal circumstances, the Park's Golden Jubilee would have been

The Jubilee Tree plaque, which is typical of numerous commemorative plaques in the Park. Photo George Ward

celebrated on or about 11 August 1918, towards the close of the First World War, but it was decided to defer the ceremony until a more appropriate time. The following account of the event appeared in the Committee Minutes of 16 September 1919:

FIFTIETH ANNIVERSARY OF THE OPENING OF THE ALBERT PARK

The Town Clerk reported that in accordance with the Resolutions of this Committee appearing on Page 881 of the printed Minutes and confirmed by the Town Council, reference was made in the Official Programme of the Peace Celebrations Festivities as to the Fiftieth Anniversary of the Opening of the Albert Park, presented to the Town of Middlesbrough by the late H W F Bolckow, Esq, First Member of Parliament for the Borough, and that in commemoration of that event, H W F Bolckow, Esq, JP, of Brackenhoe, Marton-in-Cleveland, the present representative of the original donor, planted a tree in the presence of a distinguished company of residents of Middlesbrough in the Albert Park on Saturday, the 19th July, 1919, ('Peace Celebration Day'). As a memento of the Ceremony Mr Bolckow was handed a spade upon a Silver Salver which was presented to him on behalf of the Corporation by Mrs Emanuel Spence, Wife of the Chairman of the Park Committee.

Mr Bolckow then duly planted the tree amidst great applause, and returned thanks for the honour the Corporation had done to him and his family in asking him to undertake that Ceremony. He incidentally referred to the correspondence which had recently appeared in the Local Press as to certain portions of the Park being for Games such as Tennis, Bowls, &c., and said that he felt sure that the Corporation, in setting apart portions of the Park for such Games, were fully carrying out the wishes of his Great Uncle, who was the Donor of the Park.

The Chairman of the Park Committee (Councillor E Spence) then thanked Mr Bolckow for having performed that interesting Ceremony in commemoration of the Jubilee of the Opening of the Park which took place on the 11th August 1868, and paid eloquent testimony to the generous deeds of the Bolckow family in Middlesbrough. He stated that the Park had proved to be the most noble gift which had ever been made to the Town of Middlesbrough, and that the Town Council and inhabitants of the Borough as a whole cherished the name of 'Bolckow' for that magnificent open space in which the people of Middlesbrough had been able to enjoy to the fullest extent the beautiful scenery of the Park and its surroundings, and which undoubtedly at the present time was the best lung that the Town possessed.

On this occasion, there must have been a special feeling of nostalgia for those more mature citizens who had actually been present at the opening of the Park almost fifty-one years earlier. As they listened to the words of his great-nephew, they would recall with pride the address delivered by the first Henry Bolckow to the young Prince Arthur.

From 19-27 September 1925, there were fund-raising events in Middlesbrough on behalf of local hospitals and the Park was used as one of the venues. It was also the setting for a public gathering in connection with the visit of His Royal Highness the Prince of Wales, later to become King Edward VIII, who officially opened Middlesbrough's Constantine College on 2nd July 1930. Five years later, the Silver Jubilee of his father, King George V, was commemorated in the Park.

King George VI and Queen Elizabeth (the late Queen Mother) visited the Park in 1941, an event to be described in the following section of this chapter, and the Coronation of their daughter, Queen Elizabeth II, was marked in July 1953 by the Girl Guides' Association, with the presentation of a seat for the use of visitors to the Park. On 7 June 1977, the Silver Jubilee of her accession was celebrated in the Park by the roasting of a bullock. Ken Sherwood recalls that the latter event was only partially successful because it proved to be very difficult to cook the huge beast right through to the centre.

Over and above all such events of an official, celebratory and commemorative nature, the Park has been the setting for displays and exhibitions, parades and demonstrations, musical and cultural functions, fairs and circuses, and so on. For sixty years, Albert Park was the only park in Middlesbrough, but, even though others are now available as venues for public events, its significance in this respect has been maintained.

Wartime Activities in the Park
It has already been noted that both World Wars had a direct effect on the Park workforce, in that employees there, as in all walks of life, became involved in military service. In their absence, the work of maintenance had to continue, while the Park itself was put to good use as a wartime resource, in relation to both military and civilian activities.

Military Activities
On 16 January 1917, members of the Committee agreed that the Park could be used for training purposes in relation to an obstacle course, bayonet fighting and drill. In February of the same year, permission was given for the swings to be used in bayonet training and in the following month they were hung in the Gymnasium for the same purpose. Drilling of volunteers also became a training feature and concern was expressed at the effect which this had on the grass near the band stand.

Having taken something of a battering in the War effort, the Park was the scene of celebrations on Peace Day, held on 19 July 1919. As we saw above, these were also associated with the celebration of the park's Golden Jubilee, activities including games and sports for the children. One event of particular interest was the presentation of a tank to the Mayor of Middlesbrough by Brigadier-General Blair, Commanding Officer of the Tees Garrison. The tank stood in Park Road North until 1939, when it was removed for scrap.

In January of that year, eight months before the outbreak of the Second War, Air Raid Precautions personnel were given access to the Park and they began night patrols in the April. In late September, the searchlight which had been situated on Clairville Recreation Ground, just outside the eastern boundary of the Park, was moved into the Park itself.

December 15th saw an agreement to the use of Park land as a demonstration area for the cultivation of food and this was the beginning of a very important activity which was to last for the duration. The Parks Superintendent gave regular reports on the high level of food production, which was made available for purchase by local hospitals.

On 19 April 1940, it was agreed that the Royal Air Force should install an anti-aircraft balloon in the Park, at a rental of five shillings per annum for the site, which was close to the Depot yard. In July of the same year, the Committee was asked for access to the Park for the construction of air raid shelters.

The barrage balloon was affectionately known as 'Big Bertha' and it was a source of great interest to young Ken Sherwood. The balloon was actually managed by a group of young WAAFs, for whom Ken and his mates would run errands and do little jobs. In return, the girls gave them mugs of tea and bacon sandwiches, or bread

Mrs Ethel Newton and son Gordon in 1942, with barrage balloon 'Big Bertha' in the background. Gordon Newton

dipped in the bacon fat. When the air raid sirens were sounded, the balloon was winched out, so that it could ascend and become an obstruction to German bombers heading for the local works or the docks. Speed was essential and the retaining rope would scream as it rolled rapidly off the winch.

The WAAFs were of considerable interest to slightly older young men, in the shape of American and Canadian airmen, who came bearing gifts, probably of silk stockings. Ken himself stood to gain from their visits, in that he was a keen collector of cigarette packets, of which he would find prime examples in that area. I must say that I envy him that easy task, remembering my own boyhood experiences of going head-first into litter bins on a similar quest!

The Park was closed to the public for a period in May-June 1941 after enemy action and the use of the searchlight was discontinued from 15 May. June of that year brought a request to form a new entrance into the Park from Park Road South for direct access to the barrage balloon site. At a later period in the War, Ken Sherwood arrived at work the morning after an air raid and a bomb crater was discovered in the path adjacent to the Lower Lake.

On 19 June 1941, the Park was the setting for a ceremony which was attended by Their Majesties King George VI and Queen Elizabeth. On that occasion, they inspected a parade of Civil Defence personnel and presented awards to some of these volunteers who were involved in important activities on the Home Front. There was no prior public announcement of the visit, but ARP personnel were obviously briefed. So, apparently were their families and friends, for the Park was packed. The Royal couple stayed for an hour and their presence was a real morale-booster for all involved. This was, incidentally, not actually their first visit to Middlesbrough for, as Duke and Duchess of York, they had opened the Tees Newport Bridge in February 1934.

In May 1942 the Home Guard was given permission to organise a display in the Park and in November 1944 military buildings and the balloon site were de-requisitioned. On 26 April 1946, just under a year after the cessation of hostilities, it was reported to Committee that these buildings had been removed.

During the War years, Park employees had to share the responsibility of fire-watching, which involved being present on site throughout the night. In their mess hut, they were provided with two-tier bunk beds and heating was by means of a coke-burning stove. Before their younger colleagues, Ken Sherwood and his mates, went home, they had to ensure that there was an adequate supply of sticks and a bucket of coke on stand-by for the night.

Civilian Activities
The public was still able to make regular use of the Park throughout the War periods and the Summer of 1941 saw the beginning of the Town Council's 'Holidays at Home' programmes of events, which were to continue for the duration and, re-styled 'Pleasure in Parkland', for many years after the War.

The Town Clerk presented the following report to the Parks Committee on 19 September 1941:

WARTIME HOLIDAYS AT HOME SCHEME

The Parks Committee met on July 28th and decided to organise some scheme for holidays at home and the Council at its meeting on the same day confirmed the action of the Committee in deciding to allocate a sum of £500. A visit was made to Huddersfield on the following Thursday to see what that Authority, to whose efforts a great deal of publicity had been given by the Press and the BBC, had arranged. A further Meeting was held on Thursday, August 7th, to report progress, all details being left with the Chairman and the Town Clerk.

In view of the cessation of school holidays on the 26th August, and the short time available for making arrangements, together with the difficulty in obtaining labour and materials, it was decided to concentrate on providing entertainment in the Albert Park only during the week commencing August 18th, i.e. Stockton Race Week. The Committee will appreciate that it was found impossible to arrange all that was intended - for example it might be mentioned that of five bands written to, by Tuesday prior to the aforesaid week, only one reply had been received and that was a negative one. The question of staging was also one of difficulty.

However, arrangements were made for a concert party and dance band every evening, and for the children, there was a children's concert party every afternoon, together with a Punch and Judy Show, and a ventriloquist. By far the most popular attraction, however, were roundabouts and donkeys. With a view to controlling the numbers expected to patronise these, it was decided to make a small charge, but even so, at times the crowds were unmanageable. The RAF Band performed on three afternoons, and the Cargo Fleet Ironworks Band on the Sunday afternoon.

During the week the local bowling clubs organised and ran a very successful tournament, for which there were some 400 entries. The Linthorpe Tennis Club, also organised a tennis tournament, which, whilst it did not have so many entries, provided entertainment for many spectators. The thanks of the Committee are due to all these clubs and their officials for their efforts.

The shortage of time did not permit of many special features being arranged, but the attention of all members of the Corporation was drawn to three attractions, viz.: (1) a Swimming Gala at the Baths on the Thursday afternoon, when there was a packed house; (2) a drill competition for sections of the AFS in the Park on the Friday afternoon, which had many interested spectators; and (3) First Aid demonstrations in the Park on the Tuesday evening, given by the local St John's Ambulance Brigade. Thanks are here again due to all who helped to put on these attractions.

Only one thing was not a success, judged by the interest displayed by members of the public, and that was the physical training classes, which had to be discontinued. Helped by the weather, all the other entertainments provided were well patronised and appreciated. Many people came in from the surrounding districts, even from as far as Whitby, and (according to rumour) Leeds. It was therefore decided to carry on the entertainments for an extra day, on Monday, the 25th instant.

The total cost of the scheme was £398 and the receipts amounted to £134. Nett expenditure £264.

The Park had clearly come into its own for this highly successful programme of events and the Parks Committee ordered that a similar schedule should be planned for the following year. Their Minutes of 24 September 1942 reveal an expenditure of £1,388 1s 0d and a deficit of £407 5s 2d on a series of entertainments which included a steam-powered roundabout (purchased for £150); donkeys (purchased for £55); concerts, bands, etc; Children's Concert Party, Punch and Judy Show, Ventriloquist and Clown; and Swimming Gala, Boxing, Tennis and Bowls Tournaments.

The major addition to the 1943 programme was a Scenic Railway which was purchased for £1,250, other innovations including a Circus, a Baby Competition, Livestock Competitions and a number of different displays. The overall deficit on expenditure was £1,859 4s 8d.

The scenic railway was situated in Sector 3, on the site of the Cricket Ground. It was driven by a steam engine and operated by Benny Chilvers, a retired railwayman.

The track was laid out on a circuit, but it also allowed the train to go up and down when in motion. Badly damaged by a gale in February 1948, the railway was reported to Committee as being removed by 18 June of the same year.

Nearby was the steam roundabout, on which the handsome wooden horses were hand-carved. This popular, but decaying, attraction actually survived for another four years after the demise of the scenic railway. On 25 January 1952, however, by which time it was probably about sixty years old, its poor condition led to the decision to sell it. That, however, was more easily said than done, with tenders of £250 and £100 simply falling through. Finally, on 24 October, it was confirmed that the sale had actually gone through, on a tender of £75. Within the following month, the roundabout was removed from the site.

The 1943 programme for Holidays at Home seemed to have set the trend for the remainder of the War and it is clear from detailed reports to Committee that the ensuing schemes proved to be just as popular. For example, between April and September 1945, the scenic railway was used by 26,812 adults and 102,503 children, with an income of £762 4s 11d.

In making his gift of the Park, Henry Bolckow's intention had been to provide a means of escape from the rigours, routines and, indeed, temptations of everyday life, and I feel sure that he would have firmly approved of such large-scale community use during the Second War. I wonder, however, how many of those who enjoyed these holiday activities would have felt any gratitude to him personally for the fact that they were able to be there enjoying themselves.

Chapter Six

Henry Bolckow - In Memoriam

On 8 February 1866, after the inaugural ceremony of tree-planting in the Park, and in the presence of Henry Bolckow himself, the Mayor of Middlesbrough, George Watson, had made clear his sense of gratitude to the donor in quite a dramatic way. He suggested that a statue in his honour should be erected in the most prominent position in the Park. Given that such a tribute is normally paid *post mortem*, this suggestion may well have been considered as out of place. Bearing in mind the fact that he had turned down the earlier suggestion that his name should be associated with the Park, this proposal must have embarrassed Henry Bolckow, but at least the Mayor displayed the courage of his own convictions in his proposal.

In 1873 and 1875, occasional references to the subject were made at meetings of the Park Committee, then in June of the latter year the theme was taken up by *The Dominie*, which described itself as 'a local serio-comic journal', incorporating a sketch of Bolckow on a pedestal on the summit of the Mound in the centre of the Park. For a suitable inscription on the pedestal, it was suggested that the wording should be borrowed from the tomb of Sir Christopher Wren, the creator of the new London which rose from the ashes of the Great Fire of 1666:

If you consider a monument necessary, look around.

Henry Bolckow died in 1878 and the realistic consideration of the erection of a statue in his honour was taken up by William Fallows, who was a great admirer of the man and of his achievements. Fallows himself had lived in the town since its beginning in 1830 and was regarded, in his own lifetime, as *The Father of Middlesbrough*. He chaired a committee with the objective of raising funds through public subscription. In this, the committee was successful and the unveiling of the Bolckow statue was the highlight of Middlesbrough's Jubilee Day Celebrations on 6 October 1881. The statue was actually erected on Marton Road, close to the Royal Exchange Building, which was diagonally opposite the Railway Station.

Despite this public acknowledgement of the honour due to Henry Bolckow, there was still no memorial to him in his Park and the matter re-appeared in the Committee Minutes in November 1894. A Memorial sub-committee was formed on 23 April 1895 and on 6 May of the same year it was reported that a letter on

The conjectured Bolckow Memorial of 1875. Author's Collection the subject had been received from Sir Hugh Gilzean-Reid, the proprietor of the *North Eastern Daily Gazette*. This was to express his delight at the proposal to consider the provision of a memorial to Bolckow and he stated that:

> *The time will come when his priceless service to Middlesbrough and its industries will be better understood and more thoroughly appreciated than they are today by many of the younger generation.*

This moral support for the Memorial concept was to take a much more practical turn and it was reported on 28 January 1896 that Sir Hugh had actually offered to provide a drinking fountain as a Bolckow Memorial. The evolution of the project can be traced in the Committee Minutes, the site chosen being on the south side of the main walk, east of the Curator's Lodge and close to the path leading to the Cannon Lake. A bust of Henry Bolckow was to be the centrepiece of the structure and the following was to be inscribed on the back of the Memorial itself:

HENRY WILLIAM FERDINAND BOLCKOW
Born 1806 – Died 1878

> *First Mayor (1853) and First Representative in Parliament (1868) of Middlesbrough. HENRY BOLCKOW was chief founder of its Industries; Pioneer of its Educational, Religious, and Charitable Movements; and, with generous forethought, he gave for all time, to the People of Middlesbrough this spacious Park – which was opened by Prince Arthur in 1868 – and placed over it the name of Albert the Good. To record the name of the Munificent Donor, the Fountain and Bust, presented to the Corporation by Sir Hugh Gilzean-Reid, are placed here in grateful remembrance.*
>
> *(II) This Memorial – presented to the Corporation and Inhabitants of Middlesbrough by Sir Hugh Gilzean-Reid – was designed and executed by D W Stevenson, RSA, Sculptor of the Bolckow Jubilee Statue.*

The ceremony of unveiling the Memorial was carried out by the donor himself on 30 October 1896 and the following editorial comment appeared in the *North Eastern Daily Gazette* of the 31st:

> *At length the beautiful Park at Middlesbrough is in a position to show all who visit it the name of him who presented to the town in its younger days what will ever remain one of its most valuable possessions. The ceremony of unveiling the fountain and bust, which was performed by Sir Hugh Gilzean-Reid yesterday, was the act which finally handed over to the town a commemorative monument which, while being useful in itself, is also a striking addition to the many ornamental characteristics of the Park.*

The same issue of the *Gazette* carried a long news report of the ceremony, which was described as 'an interesting and auspicious event in the history of the Albert Park', and the Memorial itself is described thus:

> *...is built of red sandstone, which is calculated to withstand the stress of weather. It is about six feet broad at the base, and rises to a height of about eleven feet. In the top half of the erection is a deep alcove in which, upon a slightly raised pedestal,*

The Bolckow Memorial Fountain near the main gates, after its removal from its original site. Author's collection

stands the splendid bust of Mr H W F Bolckow. This alcove is surmounted by a heavy cluster of leaves, while immediately below the bust is the simple inscription, 'H W F Bolckow', and in small letters below, slightly to the side, is the name of the sculptor, 'D W Stevenson, FSA' Below this is the drinking fountain, the water being emitted from the mouth of a brass lion's head, and falling into a large artificially sculptured bowl.

Even though the Bolckow Memorial had been constructed to 'withstand the stress of weather', it had not been envisaged that there would be 'any danger from human hands' (to use Hugh Gilzean-Reid's own words from a letter of 14 May 1898).

The sad fact is that the Memorial was vandalised and the Park Committee had invited the donor to become involved in discussions relating to its removal. On 30 July of that year, the Committee ordered that the drinking cups should be removed and the water cut off. By 27 June 1899, the whole structure had been removed and it was built on to the back of the wall to the south of the main entrance gates. It was subsequently moved again, presumably at the time of the reconstruction of the front walls to accommodate the War Memorial in 1922. This was to the west side of the front of the West

The Bolckow Memorial Fountain, attached to the front of the West Lodge. Photo George Ward

Lodge, but without the Bolckow bust, which is now preserved in the Mayor's Parlour in the Municipal Buildings. The original site of the Memorial itself is close to the Clock.

Following the demise of the drinking fountain Memorial, the Park Committee entered into discussions with the Bolckow family in an attempt to reach agreement on a suitable replacement for it. Initially, Carl Ferdinand Henry, the donor's nephew, was displeased when suggestions were made relating to fund-raising for a memorial by means of an Industrial Exhibition. He later suggested that an inscribed brass or marble tablet should be fixed to the main entrance gates. However, following the recommendation of the Borough Surveyor, it was agreed that a bronze tablet should be fixed to a blank wall on the Curator's Lodge. It was reported as fixed by 26 November 1901. The Park Committee Minutes do not appear to record the actual inscription on the tablet, which, incidentally, has since been removed. As we saw earlier, however, the following note appears in the Department of the Environment description of the Lodge in 1988:

...bronze tablet records:
THIS PARK WAS PRESENTED TO THE
PEOPLE OF MIDDLESBROUGH BY
HENRY WILLIAM FERDINAND BOLCKOW.
OPENED BY PRINCE ARTHUR IN 1868...

Following the restoration of the stonework into which the tablet was originally set, which has been damaged by dampness and weathering, the tablet itself is to be reinstated, the whole monument being protected from surface water by means of a newly-created pediment.

The Bolckow statue occupied its original site near the Royal Exchange until 1925, when it was removed in order to make way for the area to be laid out as a bus terminus. In October of that year, it was proposed by the Parks Committee that the statue should be re-erected in Victoria Square, where there were already statues in honour of John Vaughan and Sir Samuel Sadler, but the Bolckow family said that they would like it to be placed in Albert Park. It was duly moved to the site which is now occupied by the Crimean Cannon in the Albert Park Memorial Garden.

This was, however, not to be a permanent home for the statue. In 1985, the Royal Exchange Building was demolished, the site being re-designed as Exchange Square, and the Council deciding that the statue should be returned to its original position. I remember suggesting at the time that Henry should be left where he was and that a statue of Joseph Pease, the founder of Middlesbrough, could be commissioned and erected in Exchange Square, but to no avail. In this way, what could have been an ideal permanent home for a Bolckow Memorial in the Park which he had given to the people of Middlesbrough was lost after a period of sixty years.

What is, however, very pleasing is the fact that the Restoration Project will lead to the reinstatement of the first Bolckow Memorial in the Park – the structure which was originally Sir Hugh Gilzean-Reid's drinking fountain. The Hirst Conservation Survey revealed that its fabric has deteriorated over time, principally due to the dampness and shade of its situation. Rain water runs down the ramp which gives disabled access to the West Lodge, and from the adjacent brick wall. Algal growth

The Bolckow Statue in the Park, also showing the prehistoric tree trunk and the ancient boulder. This site is now occupied by the Crimean Cannon. Author's Collection

requires removal, but the inscription on the back of the memorial does not require attention, although it is better preserved at the top than it is at the bottom.

It has been decided that the Bolckow bust, which formerly occupied the glazed recess in the main structure, is to be moulded, replicated by using fibre glass and coloured resin, and reinstated. The fully-conserved and completed memorial will then be transferred to a prominent site. Mounted on a new base, it will then be seen and fully appreciated by all who visit the Park. As a result, no visitor will be in any doubt about the identity of Henry Bolckow, who gave the Park 'to my fellow-townsmen for the purpose of healthful recreation and exercise'.

APPENDIX 1

A Description of the Park from the *Middlesbrough & Stockton Gazette* of 14 August 1868

The gates of the park are approached from Linthorpe Road by a carriage drive, 120 feet wide at the entrance and gradually narrowing towards the gates, which furnish a beautiful specimen of iron-work, and elicited much admiration when shown at the York Industrial Exhibition last year. They are 26 feet in width and 16 feet 6 inches high, and are flanked by massive recessed winged walls, each 50 feet in length. These walls are surmounted by ornamental vases, giving the entrance to the park a very fine and finished appearance. Within the grounds, to the right of the entrance, stands the residence of Mr Cleeton, the curator, erected in the decorated style of Gothic architecture from a design by Mr C J Adams, of Stockton. The centre walk, opening from the entrance gates, is 750 feet in length, and 15 feet in width, and is planted on each side with Wellingtonias – most of which are memorial trees planted by different individuals at the invitation of Mr Bolckow – which will, in a few years, form a beautiful avenue. It is to be called the Wellingtonia Walk. Proceeding down this walk, we reach the centre mound, 96 feet across, encircled by an asphalted promenade 46 feet wide and 1,000 feet long, taking the centre of the path. The mound is planted with Rhododendrons, and kindred varieties of ornamental foliage. The outer edge of the foliage is already well planted by beds of trees and shrubs in a very forward state of growth. The main walk is continued from the opposite side of this promenade for a further distance of 1,000 feet, when it is terminated by a handsome flight of stone steps, leading to the lower lake. The walk is planted on each side with three varieties of horse chestnuts, and the steps are somewhat remarkable in their way. Each step is 12 feet long, 18 inches broad, and 6 inches deep, and is one solid block, cut from stone hewn in the neighbourhood of Halifax. Upon each side of the steps is a low stone coping and at the corners are pillars. These pillars are surmounted by vases, and these give the steps a very complete appearance.

We will now return to the entrance gates, and take a walk round the grounds. Taking the gravel walk to the left hand, we pass several beds laid out with ornamental plants and shrubs, interspersed with evergreens and trees, the most notable being some promising young Wellingtonias, and an aurcauria. The bowling green, 129 feet square, is immediately reached – which will no doubt soon afford substantial enjoyment to the admirers of that ancient and not-to-be-despised game. Owing to the remarkably dry season, the strong clayey land, and the unusually hot weather we had experienced, the ground had not yet been completed in the manner intended. It may not be generally known that this favourite British pastime was prohibited in England during the reign of Henry VIII, by Act of Parliament, and that the law was only repealed so recently as 1845. But we will proceed – Several large hawthorn bushes, remains of the 'Second Sailor's Trod', a very ancient footpath, recently diverted by Act of Parliament, are next reached, and appear under widely different circumstances to what we were accustomed to see a few years ago. They are now relics of a byegone time. Passing these, we come across six trees planted in such a manner as to form five triangles. This will be a puzzle for our young friends. The trees are a Lombardy poplar, horse chestnut, walnut, oak, elm, and acacia.

The croquet ground is next reached. It is planted round with trees and shrubs to form a retired shelter; it is very tastefully laid out, and will only possibly be found too small for the number to join in this popular game. Like the bowling green it is full of large fissures in the clay, for want of moisture. A walk across the centre of the Park from north to south now appears, and we will pursue it for a short distance. The north portion of the walk is 540 feet long, and 14 feet wide, and for the entire length is laid out upon each side, in a festooned chain border, from an original design by Mr Cleeton. Adjoining this walk upon the west side is a maze, laid out upon the famous plan of that at Hampton Court. When the hedges get up to five or six feet in height, it will be a maze indeed.

Opposite the entrance to the maze is the Swiss walk, 14 feet wide, which we will now take. It winds gracefully through some hills, planted with oak, ash, elm, poplar, &c, with a luxuriant undergrowth of shrubs. When the trees get into maturity, there will be alike a cool refuge from the sun, with sultriest beams, and a protected refuge in the winter, when 'from the north the fierce winds blow'. We next reach a circular mound planted with ornamental trees upon the top, and upon the sides with the variegated acuba japonica, producing a very fine effect. Ascending a flight of steps to the right of the walk, a winding path leads to the top of the hill – the highest point in the grounds –

> *How lovely from this hill's superior height,*
> *Spreads the wide scene before the straining sight!*

Commanding views of the whole of the park, and the surrounding landscape in every direction – the ships upon the river, railway trains passing in all directions, the ironworks of the district, Stockton with its churches, the Cleveland hills, Captain Cook's monument, Roseberry Topping, the Hambledon Hills, and the distant ocean – a magnificent panorama. Returning to the Swiss walk, we continue our way to a flight of steps leading to the archery ground, 540 feet in length and about 240 feet wide, where ladies and gentlemen may make their appearance for a contest, armed with the bow, string, arrow, glove and brace, show their proficiency in standing, knocking, drawing, holding and loosing, and their qualifications as archers by hitting the gold, red, inner-white, or black. Should any one be so unfortunate as to miss an outer-white, the embankment constructed at either end of the ground will stop the arrows – and doubtless they will sometimes be brought into requisition.

At the end of the Swiss walk, the lower lake is reached, and taking a turn to the left, and pausing upon a bridge at the northern extremity, the waterfall, nearly 30 feet wide, and about five feet in depth, will be seen to advantage, and also the lake itself. From this point, nearly the whole length is seen, and the curving banks form a very rural scene. There are two small islands near to the western side, and a large one in the centre, rising to a height of fifteen feet. It will be planted round with trees, and surmounted at the top by a quaint-looking house, intended for the accommodation of the swans, ducks and other water-fowl that may disport themselves upon the lake, the edges of which have been made of stone, for the purpose of keeping the water clean. Upon the east side of the walk round the lake is the Marton-road boundary of the park, in front of which is a low embankment, planted with trees and flowers in sorts, and a little further on there is a shady grove of willows, of luxuriant growth, where one can sit in the shade and view a portion of the park and the beautiful sheet of water spread at his feet, or turn in the opposite direction, and have an uninterrupted view of the hills in the distance. The shade of these willows will be a decidedly favourite resort of those of a meditative turn of mind, or those on 'love's errand bent'; it is a spot where they can sit 'hid from the vulgar eye' upon the grassy bank.

Crossing another bridge over the upper end of the lake there is a choice of two walks. Taking that along the southern boundary of the grounds, the visitor will be brought back to the entrance lodge. Each side of this walk is bounded with trees, one portion planted in cloud-fashion, which is very ornamental, another in sweeps, and others in mixtures. Taking the other walk from the lower lake, the cricket ground is reached. It is nearly five acres in extent, and of ample dimensions for playing the game, within a plateau twelve feet wide, and inclined six inches towards the centre, thus giving bystanders a better view of the play than if it had remained level. Upon the southern side of the walk is the exhibition ground, which is set out upon an original plan, so far as our knowledge extends. It is in the form of a terrace with four wings and a centre rising by tiers to a height of 5 feet 6 inches from the ground. The two outer sides, or tables, are 31 feet long, and 2 feet 6 inches in height; the four wings are each 54 feet long, with two tiers, respectively 2 feet 6 inches and 4 feet high, and a centre in three tiers, 2 feet 6 inches, 4 feet, and 5 feet 6 inches from the ground, with grass walks all round them. The various tiers of this show ground are built of slag, and then covered with earth, with a growth of grass, thus rendering unnecessary the deal boards generally found as flower stands at horticultural shows. Another advantage of these raised embankments is that five different sizes of tents may be used, according to the requirements of the case. For a small show, the centre would be sufficient, and for larger shows the wings might be taken in as was thought necessary. A still further advantage of the embankments is that two pic-nics can be held upon a small scale, each separated so as to be private from the other, and that treats for school children could be set out upon these natural tables to accommodate two or three thousand at once. The front and sides of the embankment are now planted with ivy, ferns, moss, polyanthuses, crocuses, primroses, periwinkle, winter aconites, snowdrops, and other dwarf-growing plants that will come in character with the rest. It will thus be seen that this show ground, when not in use, is no common ornament to the park itself. At the outer edge of the ground a number of young trees are planted, which, when grown, will effectually screen the show from the observation of outsiders. The show of the Middlesbrough Horticultural Society was held here on the 18th of August.

Leaving the show ground, we come to the centre walk across to the south side of the park. This is laid out on each side with an oval chain border, having at each end and in the centre a diamond chain, each side being 540 feet long. Following the path to the south boundary for a short distance, we turn up the 'Lover's Walk', and passing through a rustic archway, come suddenly and unexpectedly upon an ornamental lake, surrounded by a footpath, bordered with rockwork, and passing under three rustic arches. From what we hear this is thought most highly of as being a 'bit of fairy land'; almost every visitor to the park going there first. Upon the north side of the lake, we find an ancient-looking stone arch erected, in which some remains of the ancient church at Newport are introduced; as also suitable contributions by several local gentlemen. It is intended that this and the other arches shall be overgrown with ivy and various creepers. The embankments round the lake are planted with tall trees, creepers, small shrubs, climbers, &c. Specimens of the variegated Japan honeysuckle (which is generally treated as a greenhouse plant) have been growing upon the embankment here for above two years, and are doing remarkably well. Immediately facing the ancient arch before mentioned a seat is placed, so as to command a view of the water, rockwork, rustic arches, and shrubs upon the opposite side, forming a scene for a picture such as we rarely meet with. In the centre of the lake there is an island that would be a suitable resort for aquatic fowls, and these will complete the appearance of this, the most effective bit of scenery to be found in the park, and, it will be admitted, an honour to the designer and executor. Leaving this charming spot, upon the south side we reach the boundary walk, near the site of the proposed gymnasium, with which no commencement has yet been made; and then we come to the entrance gate again. The total length of walks in the park is about four miles; no adequate calculation can be made of the extent of the drainage, the pipes in some parts being only nine feet apart. At the commencement of the park it was feared it could never be got dry enough to walk upon, but that great difficulty has been overcome. The foundation of the whole of the walks is slag, an immense quantity of which has been brought into the park – upon a railway constructed for the purpose – and broken by a steam crusher, kindly supplied by the Middlesbrough Owners.

The arduous work of laying out the park has been going on for above two years; at one time more than 150 men were employed, so that the cost for labour alone must have been very heavy. The plans for the park were supplied by Mr William Barratt, landscape gardener, Wakefield; the whole work has been carried out under his instructions by Mr E Cleeton, curator, of whom Mr Barratt speaks in the highest terms. Mr Freeman, clerk of the works for Mr Bolckow's schools at Middlesbrough, designed the walls for the entrance gates, and superintended their erection. The woodwork required has been prepared by Mr Dent, Dock Street, Middlesbrough; the brickwork by Mr John Stainsby, of Middlesbrough; the stonework and steps by Mr Joseph Lord, of Middlesbrough; a portion of the wire and iron fencing by Mr S T Stephenson, of Stockton and Middlesbrough; the iron gates and a portion of the fencing by Mr Walker, of York; the asphalting by Mr Thomas Crampton, of Halifax; and the seats by Mr Dent and Mr Blakiston, of Middlesbrough. The whole of the work has been executed in a most satisfactory manner, and the trees and plants in the park are in first-class condition, but the unusually dry season has of course affected for the present the appearance of the grass and flowers, which, however, are remarkably green when all the influences they have had to contend against are taken into account. Nearly the whole of the trees, shrubs, creepers, and plants were from Mr Barratt's nurseries at Wakefield, and form a fine collection. A code of bye-laws for the proper regulation of the park has been prepared by the Town Council.

Mr Bolckow has reserved, as was done by Sir Francis Crossley, at Halifax, a strip of land round the park to be sold as building sites, for which it is admirably adapted, the object being to ensure that only houses of elegant description be built close to the park. Had no protection of this nature been made, houses of an inferior class might have been erected right up to the railings; and, for that matter, the place which is intended as a direct counteractive to drinking might have been encircled with beerhouses. The reservation is, in this respect, certainly a wise and necessary one. It may be added that when the Corporation took over the munificent gift, they undertook to keep it in order and spend about £500 yearly for this purpose. It has been laid out with admirable taste and no stinted expenditure; it would be a shame were it not preserved in a style and a spirit worthy of the donor, and those he has employed to do his work.

APPENDIX 2

A Description of the Park from the *Middlesbrough Weekly Exchange* of 10 August 1871

It is most difficult to realise the inestimable benefit that has been conferred upon the town of Middlesbrough – or, indeed upon Cleveland generally – in the magnificence of the Albert Park to the metropolis of the northern iron district. Now that the hot days of autumn are upon us, a visit to the Park reveals aspects of social enjoyment and recreation of the most pleasing nature. Take an ordinary Saturday afternoon. Streams of people enter the Park at both gates, and immediately find their way to the different points of interest which attract. Staid people enjoy a read from some favourite author in a shady retreat; nurses and children flock to the lakes to see the swans, who are just now in most beautiful plumage; lovers saunter along retired walks enjoying honeyed converse; young men make haste to the cricket-ground, which on a busy day appears too confined for the numerous games that are engaged in; and the croquet-ground becomes quite a parterre of gay costumes, rivalling the flowers in the gorgeousness of their colours. The Park is so spacious that those who are reserved and enjoy seclusion can have their tastes gratified quite as much as those who are of more social dispositions. How the privilege of a visit to the Park is valued may be gathered from the fact that on busy days, according to the estimate of Mr CLEETON, the Park-keeper, no less than 10,000 people go thither for an outing. On Sundays the walks are alive with people, who, if the pleasure depicted on their faces be any index, regard an outing in this meadowy and bowery enclosure as the one 'treat' of the week, no other being attainable in this district of restricted railway privileges and inconsiderate railway management.

The Park is, without doubt, a lung to a busy and hard-working community, and to strangers is a place well worthy of a visit. Nothing can exceed the careful manner in which it is kept, a fact which speaks well for the management of the Park committee and the Park curator, Mr CLEETON. Of course there are many adornments which the lapse of years only can supply. The trees, except in one or two cases, are of very limited growth. It is, however, satisfactory to note that already this season some 3 ft. has been added to their perpendicularity, so that in places they already present a grove-like appearance. The labyrinth appears to be quite a failure on the north side, and it will have to be re-planted. In artificial accessories progress may be reported. A beautiful octagonal iron stand for the band stand is approaching completion and is an ornament to the centre of the Park, the light columns and elegant roof giving the structure quite an oriental aspect. A new lodge is being erected at the eastern gate which, we trust, will be more commodious than the one at the western end of the Park which seems to have been erected wholly on the show principle, and is altogether unsuitable as a dwelling. Amongst requirements still needed we may name a large enclosure, or series of smaller ones, where the public may safely bide over a shower of rain when it comes on, and not run the risk of a catastrophe to the toilet at present not infrequently chronicled.

Baths, too, may be designed near the lakes, and a gymnasium on the most modern principles, might be erected on some of the large green enclosures at present reserved. No doubt the committee have all these things in mind, and intend to supply them on the well-understood economic principle of bit by bit. It is pleasant to notice that whilst the Park is made available in the fullest extent for recreational and pleasure purposes, the committee wisely keep an eye upon the expenditure which it occasions. About thirty tons of hay have been gathered within the Park this season, representing a cash saving to the town of at least £140. We see no reason why in other ways these economic notions should not have scope, as the main object of a Town Council should be to save the purses of the ratepayers. The flowers which now droop and die in thousands to the disfigurement of the beds, might be more advantageously disposed of. Finally, a recent visit to the Park has convinced us that the one great desideratum at present is a place where refreshments can be obtained. The scorching rays of an August sun have heightened immensely, in our minds, the value of gingerbeer and kindred innoxious beverages, and we would ask what is there to prevent the Parks Committee from at once providing that thirsty cricketers and other ardent cultivators of physique should have an opportunity of slaking a thirst which at times, with the sun at 100 degrees flaring full upon them and drying every tissue of the body, is hardly to be endured.

APPENDIX 3

Royal Albert Park, Middlesbrough,
from the *Middlesbrough Daily Exchange* of 18 May 1881

The few days of fine weather during last week had a wonderful effect in improving the appearance of the Royal Albert Park, Middlesbrough, and numbers of people visited this most attractive place of resort, not only from Middlesbrough, but from Stockton, Hartlepool, Darlington, and other places. With a few days of sunshine, the flowers will be all out, and the trees will be drest in their charming spring vesture of 'living green'. There have been but few additions of any moment made to the attractions of the park since last season. The sun dial near the principal entrance into Albert Park, the gift of the late Mr Bolckow, is the last striking addition that the Park Committee have had to record. It is not only an interesting but a useful object, and so great a curiosity is it regarded to be that the numbers of people who visit the park, and whose first object is to read the dial and its inscriptions, have worn away the grass at the base of the dial, a fact which leads one to make the suggestion that a railing round the base would be a great improvement, and would tend to preserve the stone structure from any risk of injury. The ingenious designer of the dial which amongst other things tells the time as it is simultaneously in London, New York and Melbourne, is Mr John Smith, of Stockton-upon-Tees. Many of the inscriptions are very quaint, and well calculated to arrest the attention. The equation table would be none the worse if it were painted, so that the figures were made more distinct.

Passing on to the southern lake we find it quite alive with different varieties of water fowl, mostly recent additions. Swans, sheldrakes (a species of duck in which both the sexes are drakes, as Mr Dixon humorously suggested at a meeting of the Council the other day), widgeons, pintails, decoy, red-headed divers, are amongst the different varieties of water fowl which now make the lake their home, and which are so much admired by the juvenile visitors to this portion of the park. The whole of the ducks, with one exception, have been presented to the park by Mr Alderman Dunning, chairman of the Park Committee. Black hambros, muscovy, and pair of wild ducks are also to be numbered amongst the water fowl. Of the birds on this lake the swans are the tamest, and we are told it is not an unusual occurrence if they are not fed at the proper time, for them to waddle up to the curator's house at the entrance to the park, and look after their breakfast for themselves. At the time of our visit the lake was rather muddy, and upon enquiry as to the cause, we were told that the supply of water was derived from the surface drainage. A great improvement could be made in this lake by widening it at the lower end which now has a stelly appearance, and looks altogether too circumscribed.

The heavy winds and gales of last winter, we regret to say, have killed a great many of the evergreens, particularly the common Portugal laurel. The Austrian pine flourishes better than any other tree in the park except the holly. In about a fortnight the park will be at its best: the lilac will soon be out, together with the flowering cherries, the rhododendrons, and the various descriptions of 'May'. The gorse is mostly killed down, but this is a plant which 'dies down' every three years, and then renews itself. The central flower border walk is doing well, and there are no less than 25,000 bedding plants to draw upon for its due ornamentation, when the time arrives. At the period of our visit the gardeners were busy trimming up the grass sward, which after the recent rains looks very fresh and charming.

In former years a great deal of fish-breeding – or pisciculture, as it is scientifically called – went on at the park under the careful superintendence of Mr Alderman Todd, but this year the lower lake is stocked, and it is not felt necessary to add to the numbers of the finny tribes that inhabit its waters. These consist of trout, grayling, and perch, and the trout, we are told, are very fine, and some of them of large size. A special spawning place is provided for the fish up stream at the head of the lake, and during last spawning season those interested in the gentle art which Isaac Walton loved so well were afforded much entertainment by watching the fishes come up, in a kind of bridal procession, two and two, to the spawning beds. A well-known Middlesbrough lover of the rod and line frequently amused himself in watching these processions, and learnt at the hands of nature lessons which he could never gather from books. There are now several boats on the lake, and in the summer season these are more and more in request. They are let out at the rate of 1s. per hour, but when they are occupied by more than four persons at a time threepence per head extra is charged. The smaller boats are in the greatest request, and on holidays especially are kept busily employed.

At the present time there is a brood of cygnets, six in number, on one of the islands of the lower lake, but as they have only recently been hatched they are jealously guarded by the parent birds. The cricket ground will not be in such good condition this year as it has been in previous seasons. This portion of the park has now no rest all the year round, for as soon as the cricketing season comes to an end the football season commences, and in this way young Middlesbrough will not allow the ground to grow under its feet.

The archery ground is now used for cricket and football. It would be an excellent plan if one part of the park could be closed to cricket each year, so as to allow the grass to grow in readiness for the next. If there were two good cricket grounds in the park this might be done, but under present arrangements it would seem as if juvenile Middlesbrough would have to be content with the accommodation as it is. The refreshment shelter house in the centre of the park is becoming yearly more appreciated. The tenant this year is Mr John Wake, the well-known confectioner of Newport-road. Strangers find the refreshment house a great convenience, and patronise the liberally provided buffet in increasing numbers. The fountain is out of repair, and otherwise would be seldom played because of the expense of the water.

The central lower avenue of trees leading from the fountain to the lake are doing well and present a thriving appearance. The trees in this avenue were re-planted some years ago when various members of the Park Committee pitched upon particular trees as test trees, and each selected the one which he thought most likely to grow in the park. Mr T H Bell chose the sycamore, Mr T L Dalkin the Turkey oak; Mr J Dunning the horse chestnut; Mr R Todd the elm; and Mr T Brentnall the oriental plane. Mr Todd's selection is making the most headway, and some of these trees made no less than five feet last summer. There is a tie between Mr Bell's and Mr Dunning's selection. The Turkey oak occupies a good position in the race, but the plane is very variable, in some cases doing well and in others not thriving as could be wished. It is amusing to hear the Park Curator relate the peculiarities of these trees, which are known to the park gardeners by the names of the persons who selected them.

In respect to the other portions of the Park it is satisfactory to find that the labyrinth will in a few years be ready for use, and that the croquet ground is in excellent condition. The Park is the most popular of any of our municipal institutions, and is also one of the most useful. It is a grand lung for a smoky town, and a visit to it at any time is a source of pleasure and delight to those who are during the day pent in close confined offices, or have to undergo the drudgery of daily toil in our large manufacturing establishments. Only a week or two ago a number of gentlemen from Sunderland went through the park and expressed their pleasure at its capaciousness and the excellent order in which everything is kept. It has indeed a wonderful advantage over the Wear-Side Park in its great size. The Sunderland 'lung' and playground is only 24 acres in extent, whilst the Albert Park is 74 acres within the fences, and includes a magnificent sheet of ornamental water.

APPENDIX 4

A Visit to the Albert – By *'A Rambler'*,
from the *Middlesbrough Daily Exchange* of 6 September 1883

The people of Middlesbrough may well be proud of their park. It was a noble gift of their pioneer MP, and as a monument to his memory it far outstrips any statue that sculptor's art could produce. The breadth of 72 acres, of which it at present consists, has been well covered with vegetation, and it grows more beautiful and more attractive every year. Any one now visiting it after a lapse of, say, ten years, would be surprised to notice the high state of cultivation to which it has attained under the management of its curator, Mr E Cleaton. I chanced to pay a visit the other day and the few notes I made may, perhaps, be of some interest to the readers of this paper.

Passing through the ornamental gates at the principal entrance, in Linthorpe-road, my attention was attracted by the curious sun-dial constructed by Mr John Smith, of Stockton, which was erected at the expense of the late Mr Bolckow, MP. The structure bears the date 1879, but I think its erection did not take place till 1880. Anyway, it must be an object of interest to visitors, not only of its correct notation of solar time, but for the quaint mottoes and proverbs which cover its face. Almost behind the dial is the tree which Mr Bolckow planted when the park was opened.

Springing from the base of the dial I noticed a flower *parterre*, 50 feet in length, filled with bedding plants and annuals, which just now are in their prime, sheltered as they are from the north wind by a thick shrubbery. There are three of these long beds, each of which look very nice. Along each side of the promenade, stretching from the entrance to the fountain, are little round beds, in each of which is planted a horse-chestnut tree, twelve feet from the centre of the terrace. Between each of these, but eight feet further from the walk, is a sycamore. These chestnuts are at present protected by young saplings, whose foliage afford shelter to the centre tree, but in time these supports will be removed, and it is believed when the chestnuts have grown and developed they will form one of the finest avenues to be seen anywhere in the North of England. Though they were only put in last autumn they are all doing well and not a dead one exists among them. So well have they succeeded that I understand it is the intention of the Park Committee this winter to continue the avenue in the same style as far as the low lake. The beds in which they are planted were formerly filled with snap-dragon, but now that pretty variety of flower is mixed with several sorts of annuals, herbaceous flowers, and bedding plants.

Diverging from the main promenade in the direction of the duck-pond, I noticed at a little distance from the shelter-house a fine specimen of the cedar of Lebanon. On the opposite side of the path have been planted the three aspens that were originally placed around the Bolckow Statue, but which here appear to have more chance of thriving. Away over the grass plot to the east are the three trees planted by the ex-Mayor, Sir Stafford Northcote, and the late Lord Cavendish, each having a suitable inscription at its foot.

On the duck-pond I noticed specimens of the sheldrake, pintail, wigeon, golden-headed diver, and red-headed diver, drake and duck of each kind, which have been placed there by Ald. Dunning, the chairman of the Park Committee. The peculiarly constructed porch which formerly stood in front of Ald. Imeson's shop, and which was presented by that gentleman to the park in the autumn of 1866, is now well covered with ivy, and thus corresponds better with its surroundings. All the banks of this lake are luxuriant with periwinkle, ivy, blackberry, wild rose, and jessamine. The golden-striped periwinkle may chiefly attract the attention of the botanical student because of the extremely beautiful marking of its leaves.

At this point I may say that I had an opportunity of inspecting the propagating houses, which occupy a somewhat secluded position to the east of the duck-pond. Last winter a new house was erected 54 ft. long, within which can be accommodated 7,000 plants. The other two houses are 42 ft. in length, and all three are heated with hot water pipes springing from an ordinary saddle-back boiler. The process of propagation from slips for next year was in full swing at the time of my visit, and when I state that there are 35,000 bedding plants – of which 20,000 are geraniums – planted out in the park every year, in addition to annuals and hardy herbaceous plants, it will be seen that the accommodation for propagation and preservation during the winter must be extensive. The curator, as my readers may perhaps be aware, keeps a good show on his borders as long as he can; but eventually a sharp frost comes to wither the blooms, and after this the plants are removed with all speed under glass, and the curator distributed among the townsfolk such as he does not require to preserve. In this way many of the poorer inhabitants obtain a display of flowering plants to brighten up their houses, which otherwise they could not procure. Coming now to the floral walk, or Italian garden, which stretches north and south through the park, I notice that it is just now in the height of perfection. At the south end there are two large beds of sub-tropical plants, exactly alike – in fact, I may remark that the beds on each side of the walk throughout are as nearly as possible counterpart of each other. In the centre of each bed is a magnificent castor oil plant, surrounded by the purple foliage of the *perella nancunencis*, or dark heath plant. This again is bordered by a layer of hamiog geraniums, outside of which are tregetas, and the azure lobelia and the delicate-hued cirastia form the outer circle. Along the borders of the path there are two descriptions of beds. Those in the centre are diamond-shaped, while oblong beds flank them on each side. In the centre beds may chiefly be noticed the peculiar foliage of the Indian shot, as well as the trentum rose geranium, the pink nose *(sic)*, the yellow geranium, the blue hygeratum, the cineraria, and the maritinum white. In every fifth bed is a specimen of the clematis Jackmani, which is now in great beauty – the plants being almost hidden in purple bloom. It is often considered by gardeners that this plant will not succeed so far north, but here is has withstood the rigours of winter for six years past, and is in better condition than ever. In one bed I noticed a layer of the golden-leaved nasturtium, which is very much admired by visitors, and is very rare in the district. Throughout the whole *parterre* the blending of colour is very good indeed, no tint being unduly prominent; but a more lavish use of white and yellow in the centre beds will probably improve their appearance. The plants are so arranged as to avoid a formal appearance, and to give the best effect to the pyramidal plants. Nearer the fountain the beds run into the diamond shape, and the myriad hues of the other flowers named above are relieved by the distribution Crystal Palace gem lobelias and dark verbenas, with a groundwork of featherfoil. In another bed I noticed a rich collection of single dahlias, a return to the old style of flower that seems to be coming more and more into fashion. Around the fountain are four crescent-shaped beds, in which yellow forms the centre, flanked by blue and white, with a groundwork of pale green foliage. Passing the fountain, the visitor comes to a display which partakes more of the sub-tropical style of gardening, which is much admired. First are eight 'stroll' beds, which have a fine effect, Then there are two small round beds, and succeeding these are two large kidney-shaped beds, in the centre of which are the *accacia lopantha* and the Australian gum tree (a plant which possesses the virtue of preventing fever in malarial districts), surrounded by dahlias, petunias, Indian shot, etc. These plants, being of a delicate nature, are removed into the greenhouse during the winter. Passing these beds the visitor comes next to a Maltese cross, prominent in which is the *antimari diacra*, or 'snow in summer'. After a bed of rhododendrons there are other beds containing the *perella nancunensis*; the bijou geranium, yellow tregertis, scarlet geranium and azure lobelia, mixed with cockspur grass and 'funkies'. There are other two beds on each side, in the centre of which is the *ageratum Mexicani*, flanked by white, scarlet and bijou geraniums. Here, let me say in passing, that the 'maze' is growing well, the hedges being now of a good height, and it is probable that next spring it may be ready for the admission of visitors, who may choose to lose themselves in its perplexing intricacies.

Turning now to the east, I find on the north side of the park an ornamental lake that was made five or six years ago, and around which the trees are growing well. A short distance off there is the new gymnasium, consisting of a series of swings, a horizontal bar, and a trapeze. This form of amusement has become a great attraction to youths and boys, who crowd around the rings all day, and would be willing to extend their gymnastic performances on Sundays, if the Park Committee would allow them. To my mind, the gymnasium is the most incongruous feature I have met with in the park. It is so essentially an artificial contrivance, and forms such a focus for all the 'roughs' of the neighbourhood, that it greatly detracts from the rural simplicity which pervades nearly every other part of the park, and it is almost a pity that the Park Committee have approved it. Otherwise, there is plenty of scope in the park for amusement, for there are grounds for cricket, football, lawn tennis, and bowls, while boating and fishing can be had on the large lake. The boating is popular, and earns a modest little revenue for the committee. Fishing is more extensive than when first the licenses were granted. In the large lake some well-grown perch can be obtained, and also a few grayling, but not many trout. In the north lake, where fishing with ground-bait is allowed, some fine eels have lately been caught.

Following the path which leads past the base of the mound, the visitor enters a narrow defile, the artificial nature of which is now concealed by the thick and tangled shrubbery that clothes its banks. The shrubbery, in fact, is too thick for proper cultivation of ornamental trees, and the willows and poplars will next spring have to be cut away to give air and light to the timber trees which are springing up here and there. The willows and poplars had served their day and generation by providing shelter from the cold north winds for the young oaks, ashes, sycamores, and chestnuts that abound here, and these having become sufficiently well established, they are now able to dispense with their nursing. At the same time all the evergreen shrubs will be encouraged, especially the Austrian pine, which succeeds here capitally. Coming down to the east lake, I noticed that the committee have laid a new asphalte pavement from the north entrance to the promenade steps, and I understand it is in contemplation to continue the same course round the west side as far as Mr Chapman's house, and along the centre avenue that crosses the park from south to north. This, of course, will involve somewhat serious cost, and it is possible that this consideration may delay for a time the intentions of the Park Committee. Of course, if this improvement is carried out, it will make a splendid promenade for visitors, and will also be a good track for the bicyclists, who come down between six a.m. and nine a.m. to take their morning exercise. At the south east corner of the park I came across a nice specimen of the Thugia, or *cupressus Lawsoniana*, which is worthy of admiration. Here also a new improvement took my attention. From the floral border to the south-east corner, and round to the flagstaff, a row of young elms and planes alternately have been planted. Each has a drain from its roots to carry off surplus water, the ground here being rather too moist for successful cultivation. These trees were put in last winter, and are now looking remarkably well; in the course of a few years they will form a fine avenue that by its shade will add to the attractions of the park on a sultry day. I believe this attraction was due to a suggestion from Ald. Dunning, whose interest in all that concerns the park is well known. In what was once intended to be the show ground – a series of natural banks for the exhibition of flowering plants – nature has now been allowed to run wild. The American parsley, with its huge thick stems, that grows rapidly and as rapidly withers and dies, is here rank and luxuriant, and the underwood of the forest has filled up every vacant space between the trees till the vegetation represents the appearance of a compact mass. Of course, this crowding has its uses, for the rubbish serves to protect the valuable young plants that are here and there to be found. Some fine young Austrian pines I noticed in a promising condition, and the *cupressus Lawsoniana* is represented by several specimens. The purple beech stands sentinel at each end of the defile, and varies with its dark foliage the everlasting green that prevails around. What excited my interest to the greatest degree, however, was the maiden-hair tree – a plant the leaves of which resemble those of the maiden-hair fern, but which attains the height of 30 feet. The specimen which I saw – and there are only two in the Park – has grown fifteen inches this summer, and is now fully a yard high. All over the park the trees abound in large numbers, and in fact are almost over-abundant. Most of the trees which exist, however, have been grown on the spot, and are therefore not likely to take much harm from the soot and smoke which prevails. The dark Italian poplars and Lombardy poplars which form the fringe, as it were, round the outer edge of the park, are thriving apace, and seem to accommodate themselves to the atmosphere and temperature very well. Altogether, the park just now is in capital order – thanks to the close supervision which it receives at the hands of Mr Cleaton – and it is well worthy of a visit from any stranger who may sojourn in the town. Of course, it is taken for granted that the residents of Middlesbrough enjoy to the full the varied beauties and amusements which the park affords; but if there are any who have not recently found their way thitherwards, or who, when there, have not known where to find its most interesting features, it is to be hoped that these cursory notes will induce them to pay more frequent visits, and will enable them to understand more fully the botanical specimens which, by their rarity or their peculiar formations, add to the interest which any intelligent man will take in such a pretty place of popular resort.

Index

Norman Moorsom was born in Middlesbrough and educated at Middlesbrough Boys' High School and St John's College of Education in York. He taught for ten years in comprehensive schools around Middlesbrough, and was then appointed as Museum Schools Service Officer for the County Borough of Teesside, a post he held for over sixteen years. He then became Local History Officer for Cleveland County Council, taking early retirement in 1993. Since 1963, Norman has written thirty-five booklets and books about the Middlesbrough area. He enjoys giving lectures on local history, as well as taking guided walks around the area of the original town. He is a founder member of the Cleveland and Teesside Local History Society, established in 1968, and chairman of Middlesbrough Heritage Group. He met his wife, Sylvia when she was Senior Assistant at Middlesbrough Reference Library where much of his early research took place. They have a son, Richard, a daughter, Hilary, and two grandchildren, Laura and Andrew.